Sonnets
of the English Renaissance

Sonnets of the English Renaissance

selected and edited by
J. W. LEVER

UNIVERSITY OF LONDON
THE ATHLONE PRESS
1974

Published by
THE ATHLONE PRESS
UNIVERSITY OF LONDON
at 4 Gower Street, London WC1

Distributed by
Tiptree Book Services Ltd
Tiptree, Essex

U.S.A. and Canada
Humanities Press Inc
New York

© *J. W. Lever* 1974

0 485 13604 X *cloth*
0 485 12604 4 *paperback*

Printed in Great Britain by
WESTERN PRINTING SERVICES LTD
BRISTOL

PREFACE

These sonnets range over about a hundred years of English history, from the Reformation to the Civil War. Culturally the period had such underlying continuity and such close links with contemporary Europe that it may best be described as the English Renaissance. The aim of this volume is to show something of that diversity in unity by making comparison more easy between sonnets that are readily available in anthologies and others which are only accessible in scholarly editions devoted to individual poets. Accordingly uniform modern spelling and punctuation are employed throughout. Where readings are disputable, the versions on which my text is based are provided in the notes. Arabic numerals indicate the order of the sonnets in the present selection; where these were originally part of a numbered sequence, their place is shown by the addition of Roman numerals in brackets.

I am obviously in debt to the work of many scholars and editors past and present, to whom I tender my gratitude. Even where my readings or interpretations differ, these could not have been arrived at without their labours. I would especially mention my dependence upon the only edition of the sonnets of Alabaster, by Professors G. M. Story and Helen Gardner. However I am alone responsible for the version of the text of the ten sonnets I have chosen to represent this poet, and here as elsewhere the modernised spelling and punctuation are my own. My greatest indebtedness is to Professor Geoffrey Bullough, the General Editor of the series and editor of the poems of Fulke Greville, for his help and advice at every stage in the preparation of this collection.

J.W.L.

CONTENTS

INTRODUCTION

Let sea-discoverers to new worlds have gone,
Let maps to others, worlds on worlds have shown,
Let us possess one world, each hath one, and is one.
                              Donne, *The Good-Morrow*

Donne's lines vividly recall the eagerness of his age to explore both the outer and inner worlds of man. Through the sixteenth century, travels and voyages, the mapping of a new continent and the scanning of the moon and stars had broadened the horizons of space. With this went an ever-widening rediscovery of the past through history and archaeology, the rehabilitation of pagan myths and ancient philosophies. Just as significant as the opening out of space and time was the probing of hidden recesses of personality. Traditional categories of the psyche, though still preserved, could no longer be simply reaffirmed. The age required that they be tested on the sounding-board of individual experience, which became increasingly the measure of truth. Hence the task of comprehending the 'little world of man', which had been primarily the function of priest and scholar, came to devolve upon artist and poet.

It is in this role that the Renaissance sonnet, practised by almost every serious writer of the time, may be best understood. As a succinct, fourteen-line poem the sonnet served many purposes. Frequently it was used for dedications, formal eulogies, or political and moral epigrams. It could express amity or antipathy, and several examples of such uses are included in the present selection. But its essential function was to chart the intimacies of personal experience. Here its very limitations gave it strength. Unlike epic and drama, which presented a wide range of characters, it could investigate selfhood at the nodal point where intellect and passion, desire and spiritual aspiration intersect. Instead of tracing a panorama of action or building up a cumulative effect in time, it chose to survey internal landscapes and penetrate the moment. Other kinds of lyric might also convey a sense of immediacy and variety of mood. But through the intricacy of its structure and the tightness of its form the sonnet promoted a special degree of intensity and complexity.

Different national literatures and individual poets produced their own modifications of the sonnet's design. But the basic pattern of the Italian Renaissance was the prototype of them all and has a singular vitality which persists to this day. The verse-form consists of fourteen lines of eleven syllables, arranged in two unequal parts, making up an octave and sestet (eight lines and six), with balancing subdivisions of four lines and three. The octave, built on a peculiar scheme of two rhymes—*abba abba*—traces a sinuous movement, progressing and harking back upon itself, so that exposition and emphasis, thought and emotion, are knit together. In the sestet a rather more flexible pattern of three new rhymes, sometimes of two—*cde cde, cde dce,* or *cdc dcd,* etc.—serves to correlate the perceptions of the octave. The degree of complexity the form was made to carry differed from writer to writer and poem to poem. But in its essential function the Italian sonnet embodied a dual thought-process of perception and cognition which could reflect, with remarkable precision, the tensions and contrarieties of experience.

While most verse forms of the Renaissance were developed from classical or medieval precedents, the sonnet was the creation of its age. A rudimentary design has been traced back to thirteenth-century Sicily, but Dante and his contemporaries were the first major poets to grasp its potentialities. Their sonnets, marked by a rapt, visionary quality described in its time as the *dolce stil nuovo* ('sweet new style'), voiced a sublimated love verging on adoration, yet significantly directed towards a human being—the 'angelic lady' who inspired the poet's verse and purified his soul. But it was Petrarch a generation later who stood at the fountain head of the Renaissance sonnet. Pioneer scholar, traveller, lover and poet, combining intellectual curiosity with deeply sensuous responses, Petrarch was the forerunner of a new age. In sonnets composed over thirty years of devotion to Laura in her life and after her death, he brought together a wide range of attitudes, from the erotic hopes and frustrations of Provençal verse to the spiritual reaches of the Florentines. Through more than three hundred sonnets interspersed with lyrics in a variety of forms, his poetry evoked a love oscillating between worship and desire which involved every level of per-

sonality. Inner states of consciousness found objective corres-
pondences in the world of nature, the forces of great rivers and
stormy seas, the instinctive urges of birds and beasts, the gentle-
ness and rage of the seasons. Instead of making up a narrative
sequence, the sonnets were projections from a single core of
experience, tracing kaleidoscopic patterns of thought and feeling.
Ranging from comparatively light conceits or rhetorical tropes
to complex feats of the imagination, Petrarch's sonnets in their
totality made up a work that was to shape the poetic sensibility
of Europe for over two centuries.

Modern conceptions of personal poetry may be grossly mis-
leading as an approach to the Renaissance sonnet. This had little
concern with autobiographical detail or realistic characterisation.
It was preoccupied with an over-riding, all-important engage-
ment of the self with an other; hence with the exploration of a
polarity. That 'other' might stand in the position of mistress,
friend, or even godhead; in any case a relationship was created
which drew into its magnetic field the poet's whole personality;
his sense of his environment; his response to nature, time and
mutability; his political, religious or philosophical beliefs. More-
over poetry itself, however personal, was seen as a way of mediat-
ing experiences that all could share. The reader was not expected
to learn a secret idiom or guess at the meaning of a set of private
symbols. Just as the Renaissance painter expressed his vision
through familiar motifs from the bible or classical mythology,
each with its appropriate gesture or stance, so the poet worked
through the traditional descriptions, situations and images of
romance. The golden hair, ruby lips, radiant smile of the sonnet
heroine suggested a type of beauty, not an individual portrait,
just as her cruel chastity offered a type of feminine virtue, not a
characterisation. Such topics as the lover's solitude in spring,
his dreams in the night, the comparison of his state to that of a
hunter seeking an elusive hind, or a storm-tossed ship driven
upon the rocks, were handled and re-handled by a succession of
poets. For some, convention simply provided a model on which to
practice eloquence or ingenuity. Others re-created the traditional
themes, charging them with their own poetic power. Imitations
of this kind were in the highest degree original.

Petrarch's sonnets, themselves drawing upon convention, were
in turn 'imitated', first in Italian, later in all the languages of

western Europe. During the *quattrocento* ingenuity was the fashion, stimulated by the facile prettiness of anacreontic verse. The paradoxes of love, its 'hot ice' and 'freezing fire', the pranks of the boy Cupid, were celebrated in a variety of witty or sentimental conceits. But in the sixteenth century, with its religious and social upheavals, a new seriousness prevailed and the authentic qualities of the sonnet were rediscovered. The poets of the French *Pléiade*, especially Du Bellay and Ronsard, charged it with a fresh grace and poignancy. Petrarch's intensity was not repeated, but there was an acute awareness of the beauty and transiency of love and life itself. A generation later Tasso blended classical discipline with a strain of Platonic idealism. Decorative excrescences were cut away, and the best Italian sonnets in the new mode were in the true succession of Petrarch. Towards the end of the century a major shift of sensibility began to transform the sonnet's traditional themes. Both the Catholic and the Reformed creeds were stressing the primary importance of the individual's quest for God. Meditation and self-examination were cultivated as a spiritual discipline, which found expression in sonnets substituting the figure of Christ for that of the mistress and exploring the predicaments not of the scorned lover but the sinner in search of salvation. Towards the end of his life, sick and suffering, Ronsard dictated his last sonnets of devotion:

> Quoi, mon âme, dors-tu engourdie en ta masse?
> La trompette a sonné, serre bagage, et va
> Le chemin déserté que Jésus Christ trouva,
> Quand tout mouillé de sang racheta notre race.

The theme was taken up in a new idiom by La Ceppède and Sponde, whose curt elliptical style, abrupt questionings and startling conceits anticipated the manner, as their themes did the matter, of the English Metaphysicals.

All these developments left their mark on the sonnets of the English Renaissance. From the pioneer renderings of Petrarch by the court poets of Henry VIII, through the sonnet-sequences of the great Elizabethans, to the devotional poems of Alabaster and Donne, every European trend was reflected. Yet this impressive body of verse remained distinctively English in its temper, form, and outlook.

George Puttenham in *The Art of English Poesy* (1589) gave

lavish praise to the verse of Sir Thomas Wyatt (1503–1542) and
Henry Howard, Earl of Surrey (1515–1546): 'the two chief
lanterns of light to all others that have since employed their
pens upon English poesy, their conceits were lofty, their styles
stately, their conveyance cleanly, their terms proper, their metre
sweet and well proportioned, in all imitating very naturally and
studiously their master Francis Petrarcha'. This estimate tends
to stress what the Elizabethans were seeking rather than what
they found. Besides differing widely as individuals in their
manner and style, neither Wyatt nor Surrey wrote sonnets at all
comparable with those of Petrarch. Yet it is true that between
them they laid the foundations of the English sonnet, with its
characteristic structure and mode of expression. Of the two,
Wyatt was the more outstanding poet. The sonnets, like the rest
of his writings, are stamped with his personality and shaped by
his stormy, eventful career. Henry VIII's court was that of a
typical Renaissance despotism, combining magnificence and
ruthlessness, delight in artistic accomplishment and unscrupulous
egotism in the pursuit of power. As a handsome, talented young
man, Wyatt at first won favour. Later he fell under suspicion,
was thrice imprisoned, and witnessed the execution of his friends,
whose fate he nearly shared. Understandably his verse changed
with his life, developing from graceful erotic trifles to highly
individual love poems, complaints against the vicissitudes of
court, and penitential psalms. Tradition required that the sonnet,
which he practised for many years, be centred upon the ex-
perience of romantic love. Wyatt preserved the traditional
themes; but he subtly modified their tone and implications. As an
innovator he began with Italian models, turning for the most
part directly to Petrarch rather than his followers; yet as soon as
he had devised a suitable English form he made the sonnet voice
his own outlook and experience.

A well-known and striking example of Wyatt's method is his
sonnet 'Whoso list to hunt' (1), based on Petrarch's 'Una candida
cerva'. Anticipating Laura's death, Petrarch wrote of a white
hind that appeared before him in the meadow; how he gazed on
it through a spring morning until, about noon, it vanished. The
beloved was symbolically presented as an apparition of gentleness
and beauty, soon to disappear from the earth. Wyatt's rendering
is totally different in spirit. He sees himself as taking part, with

others, in a strenuous time-wasting hunt after an elusive court lady who belongs to 'Caesar', and is wild to hold though she seems tame. It is not unlikely that the mistress here was Anne Boleyn, with whom Wyatt had been intimate until she was appropriated by the king. A similar frankness and forcefulness shapes most of Wyatt's mature sonnets. Not only the changing fancies of women but the tricks of fortune at the Tudor court provided themes for sonnets. The traditional lover's complaint at solitude amid May Day rejoicings (3) offers a pretext for reference to Wyatt's imprisonment for the third time in May. Petrarch's elegy at the double loss of Laura and his friend Colonna becomes a lament at the fall of Thomas Cromwell, Wyatt's patron and protector (6). In 'Divers doth use' (5) he smiles at those who mourn when their ladies grow cold: it is natural for women to be fickle. These sonnets lack the high imagination and resonance of the Italian mode. They substitute plain words for eloquence, direct statement for allusiveness, pragmatic reasoning for visionary breadth. The Elizabethans would range more widely; but these qualities would persist even in their greatest verse.

To have made the Petrarchan sonnet form into an English medium was itself a remarkable achievement. The native verse tradition relied far more than Italian on stress patterns. Direct translation produced awkward switchback effects instead of Petrarch's easy flow. Instead, a staple five-foot line which incorporated stress without metrical disturbance was made the equivalent to the Italian line of eleven syllables. The verse structure too came to differ from Petrarch's and other Italian variants. In the octave, though Wyatt usually kept the rhyme-scheme *abba abba*, the subdivisions were more clearly marked off by syntax as separate quatrain units. In the sestet a separation of quatrain and couplet was similarly established. The effect of the distinct verse units and clinching final couplet was a more pointed, logically balanced statement promoting sequential reasoning rather than the intuitive apprehension of the Italian. In metre, in diction, and in content, Wyatt took the decisive steps to the establishment of the Elizabethan sonnet as an independent form.

Surrey was to continue after his own fashion the work of his older contemporary. In poetry and in life the two writers were linked by ties of friendship, common intellectual interests and

similar vicissitudes at court. Surrey too underwent spells of im-
prisonment and was executed at the age of thirty-one. But there
was a marked difference in their poetic approach. Surrey was not
primarily a writer of lyrics. His most important work was the
development of English blank verse as a narrative medium, in
which he translated two books of Virgil's *Aeneid*. He also ex-
perimented with the sonnet, but the theme of romantic love
called forth no genuine inner response. Nevertheless he was far
from insensitive; in particular he had a strong capacity for
friendship and a delight in an active soldierly life. His true gift
appears in the few sonnets where, breaking from romance
tradition, he wrote of simple affections and loyalties, or voiced his
detestation of court intrigue. Here the English form of sonnet,
with its clear-cut appositions and contrasts, served him well.
He carried Wyatt's developments further, evolving a rhyme-
scheme with three distinct quatrains of alternating rhymes,
followed by a couplet: *abab cdcd efef gg*. The form was highly
effective in such sonnets as the tribute to Wyatt, 'Divers thy death
do diversely bemoan' (2), where the hypocrisies of Wyatt's false
friends, described in the first two quatrains, are sharply juxtaposed
to Surrey's deep personal grief, compressed with cumulative
force into the third quatrain and couplet. Even more effective is
the ending of the epitaph to Thomas Clere, Surrey's comrade-
in-arms who died of wounds incurred while defending him in
battle:

> Ah Clere, if love had booted, care, or cost,
> Heaven had not won, nor earth so timely lost. (4)

In Tottel's anthology *Songs and Sonets* (1557) the verse of Wyatt
and Surrey, buried in manuscripts during their lifetimes, was
published and made available for a new generation of readers.
The collection went through five editions up to 1578, bridging
the gap between the Tudor innovators and the great Elizabethans.
Nearly all the sonnets in Tottel followed the English form, which
became the staple pattern through the Elizabethan age. Wyatt
and Surrey had also set the precedent for a use of plain, frequently
monosyllabic words, which drew their strength from the Anglo-
Saxon roots of the language. Individual poets would make their
own departures from the Tudor model, or seek to combine with it
some of the qualities they found in Italian or French sonnets; it
was a many-purpose medium rather than a strict formula. But

Wyatt and Surrey between them effectively freed the English sonnet from mere subservience to continental modes, and enabled the major Elizabethan poets to build on this groundwork their own complex structures of imagination.

The first important creation of the new age was *Astrophel and Stella* by Sir Philip Sidney (1554–1586). Composed probably in 1581–82, this sequence of 108 sonnets interspersed, in the Petrarchan manner, with lyrics in different forms, made a startling impact on a whole generation of readers. Sidney was hailed as the 'English Petrarch'—a title which, however misleading in the literal sense, at least pointed up the co-presence in his sonnets of contemporary English attitudes and the traditional Petrarchan experience. Modes of expression which, by dint of repetition over two centuries, had become as fixed and sterile as pressed flowers, were suddenly revived. For the first time Elizabethan readers were confronted with a poetic treatment of personality which breathed the spirit of their own time, spoke in their accents, shared their concerns,—yet retraced in sonnet after sonnet the ironies and ardours of romance.

Like all Renaissance sequences, *Astrophel and Stella* is not a realistic autobiography. The title itself, with its symbolic names ('Star-lover' and 'Star') implies a poetic transmutation of the hero and heroine. Conventional topics are re-handled—addresses to the moon, invocations of sleep and dreams, laments at absence, praise of the lady's 'unique' beauty and virtue, reproaches of her cold chastity, affirmations of frustrated desire. Stock conceits crop up in easily recognisable form. Even Sidney's energetic disclaimers of artifice and borrowed eloquence are framed in highly self-conscious tropes. Yet there is no mistaking the force of authentic experience that drives through the sequence. The original of 'Stella', Penelope Devereux, had been proposed as a bride for Philip Sidney when both were almost children. His parents, ambitious for a higher-ranking match, had declined the offer, and Sidney himself, a studious youth, had not shown much concern. Some years later he met her again when she was already promised in marriage to the singularly unattractive Lord Rich. Too late he found himself falling in love. The sonnets voice Sidney's desires, regrets, conflicts of conscience and bafflement in a genuine situation created by the social pressures and moral restraints of the time.

It has been said that 'Astrophel' and 'Stella' should be seen as fictitious *personae* deliberately set apart from the historical Sidney and Penelope. This guards against too literal an approach; but the dichotomy can be over-stressed. The important distinction is not between fiction and fact, but between the conflicting aspects of Sidney's personality. The conscious craftsman of verse, the sophisticated courtier and scholar, must come to terms with the infatuation that grips him. This inherent tension underlies the interplay of traditional and contemporary attitudes, from witty conceit to anguished self-searching, from the formulation of moral dilemmas to urgent calls for sexual relief. The effect is to promote a poetry of paradox sprung from the basic predicament in which Sidney found himself.

Here lies the originality of the opening sonnet, 'Loving in truth, and fain my love to show' (1). Writing in stately alexandrines, making careful use of rhetorical tropes, Sidney describes how he resorted to every aid to composition, 'studying inventions fine', 'oft turning others' leaves'. But the confidence and deliberateness fall away in the sestet, to be replaced by a growing sense of impotence that mounts to the climax and sudden reversal of the couplet:

> Biting my truant pen, beating myself for spite,
> 'Fool,' said my Muse to me, 'look in thy heart and write'.

What then should he write? Just what he has already written. The poem about composing a love-sonnet has in the process become one. Through honest self-examination Sidney has indeed looked in his heart, and in the event the literary artifice of 'study', sterile in itself, is joined to the spontaneity of 'nature'. A similar honesty everywhere revitalizes traditional attitudes. 'Not at first sight' (2) affirms, in the teeth of convention, that love grew slowly and hesitantly; yet the poet of the new age is just as inexorably love's victim as any hero of romance. The comparison of his state to that of 'slave-born Muscovite' is fully contemporary, based on recent travellers' reports, though the condition described is identical with that of ancient lovers who saw themselves as vassals of Eros. Sidney delights in adapting to sixteenth-century reality the anacreontic fables of Cupid the mischievous child. The boy god becomes a Greek refugee from the Turks (5), or a highwayman with a musket (10). Such conceits are presented with zest and a wit exercised at the writer's own expense. Sidney anticipates Shakespearean drama in the counterpointing of humour and romance. In these sonnets the smitten lover and the alert, self-critical poet are combined in one person; Sidney is, as it were, Mercutio to his own Romeo.

As the sequence proceeds the issues become graver and the emotional conflicts more acute. Sidney's sexuality is frankly admitted in the midst of his idealising; yet the idealism, too, is sincere enough. He is the product of his Protestant training and Platonist education; on a rational level he concedes that his passion is vain and self-destructive. There is a brief phase of jubilation when Stella tells him that she returns his love. She permits a kiss, but seemingly no more, though his fancy races ahead to a consummation both longed for and feared:

> what help then in my case?
> But with short breath, long looks, stayed feet, and walking head,
> Pray that my sun go down with meeker beams to bed. (30)

In effect, the courtship brings no lasting satisfaction. After a secret rendezvous where, it is hinted, he is for once allowed to have his will, there is a long separation accompanied by new laments (36–48). Finally he takes formal leave of Stella to follow an unspecified 'great cause, which needs both use and art' (42). The last sonnet of the sequence is set in a minor key, and the old editorial practice of including the two unclassified sonnets 'Thou blind man's mark' and 'Leave me, O love' has no textual authority to support it. Nevertheless these palinodes renouncing desire in favour of virtue, and 'love which reachest but to dust' in hope of 'eternal love', provide an impressive comment on the experiences of the sequence.

While a sketchy 'plot' may be traced, *Astrophel and Stella* is, like other sonnet sequences, primarily a treatment of attitudes and states of mind. Some of the poems are addressed to Stella; some are, as it were, soliloquies; some confide in an unnamed friend; some are almost versified footnotes to Sidney's theories of composition. Yet all are centred on a single all-absorbing experience. Hence the sonnet has its own inherent order and line of development. Sidney shows no concern for time as an element in the courtship; as David Kalstone has written, 'he chooses to ride on the dial's point of the moment'.[1] The experience of psychic

[1] David Kalstone, *Sidney's Poetry: Contexts and Interpretations* (1965), p. 122.

upheaval that he traces is unconscious of the objective processes of time and change, save as an intrusion from the outside world. Nor can its conflicts be sublimated into a revelation of ideal or spiritual truth. Hence the sonnets, whatever claims they make for Stella's beauty or virtue, fail to reflect Petrarch's transcendental vision. They have the egotism and immediacy of Wyatt's poetry, with a subtler degree of sophistication and mental agility. Desire is perpetually at war with reason, nature with nurture, and the unresting play of paradox is an essential part of the sonnet structure./Sidney uses a remarkable variety of rhyme-schemes; yet these most typically resolve themselves into modifications of Wyatt's form. They amount to an octave bound together by some system of interlacing rhymes, followed by a sestet where the rhyme-pattern as such is completed in four lines, yet the syntax leads the reader on to a final couplet which, instead of clinching the argument, presents instead a surprise discovery or unexpected contradiction:

> And, not content to be perfection's heir
>> Thyself, dost strive all minds that way to move
>> Who mark in thee what is in thee most fair.
> So, while thy beauty draws the heart to love,
>> As fast thy virtue bends that love to good:
>> Bu ah, desire still cries, 'Give me some food'. (28)

While the punctuation divides the verse into two tercets, the rhyme-scheme sets up units of four lines and two. Tension thus comes to centre on the last line, which hovers between its function of completing the second balancing tercet, and making up a couplet with some statement of its own. The outcome is an explosive contradiction of both modes of asserting Stella's influence. A vital paradox is launched which proves to be the unsuspected motivation of the whole poem.

Astrophel and Stella is charged with this intellectual energy. No other sonnet sequence in English so vividly projects the ardours and frustrations of sexual love in its impact on a brilliant, many-sided young man. Nor had any previous literary work in English created a lover so distinct and memorable as Sidney's Astrophel, a 'speaking picture' of his age, whose every tone and inflection of voice proclaimed his vital personality.

The *Amoretti* sequence of Edmund Spenser (1552?–1599),

published with the marriage ode *Epithalamion* in 1595, makes a very different impression on the reader. These eighty-nine sonnets with their close-patterned alliteration and interlinked rhymes seem especially designed to mute the discords of immediate experience and impose an over-riding harmony. Desire, frustration, and deferred hope—the concomitants of romance love—are cushioned through the formal weakening of the quatrain units by an unbroken rhyme-scheme—*abab bcbc cdcd*—ending with a couplet *ee* which serves to round off the exposition rather than point up inherent contrasts. The sonnets thus tend to resemble fourteen-line Spenserian stanzas, parts of a composite poem in which all direct experience is taken up into a wider reality shaped by the writer's total ethical outlook. Hence no individual sonnet makes as striking an impact as many of Sidney's. Yet the sequence as a whole bespeaks an emotional maturity beyond that of *Astrophel and Stella*. Spenser was over forty at the time of his suit to Elizabeth Boyle; most of *The Faerie Queene* as we have it had already been composed; and the vicissitudes of courtship had already found expression as one of its major themes.

Love therefore brought no serious upset to the tenor of his life. Courtship was understood as a process which, like any other in nature or the soul, must gradually come to fruition. Its contrarieties and delays were to be accepted as a form of psychic discipline, for 'never aught was excellent assayed / which was not hard t'achieve and bring to end' (16). The *Amoretti* present the working out of this process to a sacramental union, and though, like *Astrophel and Stella*, they end on a minor key, they are followed by the triumphant coda of *Epithalamion*, Spenser's own marriage song.

In keeping with this approach, the sequence incorporates into its structure time and the seasons. After three introductory sonnets, New Year is announced, with hopes of 'fresh Love' after 'sad winter's night' (4). In 9 the song of 'The merry cuckoo, messenger of spring' is heard; but the lady does not yet respond like other lovers who 'wait upon their king'. In 10, 'This holy season fit to fast and pray', Lent is taken as the time for a sacrifice of the heart; and, a good deal later on, the completion of a year of 'long languishment' is commemorated (19). This is followed in 21 by mention of a second new year, bringing hope of a change of 'minds and former lives'. 'Most glorious Lord of life' (25) celebrates Easter with an injunction to make earthly love a fulfilment of the divine precept:

> So let us love, dear love, like as we ought;
> love is the lesson which the Lord us taught.

Finally in 'Fresh spring, the herald of love's mighty king' (26) the poet calls on the lady this time to join in the rites of the king of May. Two new years, two Easter seasons, and two springs are thus set over against one another as contrasted periods of hope and promise, the latter fully realised in the marriage rejoicings of *Epithalamion*, written for Spenser's wedding day of 10 June 1594.[2] Consistently with this structuring of time, the sonnets do not allude to any summer or autumn occasions in the first calendar year, since these would have no counterparts in the second year after the period of courtship was concluded. What the sequence presents is a measured ordering of experience, proceeding on both the natural and the spiritual planes, from the sublimated ardours of wooing to the easier, more familiar and human relationship of betrothal, looking ahead in turn to the consummation and sacrament of marriage.

To some modern readers this ordering of emotional life may seem 'conventional', if not complacent. It must be recognised, though, that the very composition of love sonnets to one's future wife was, in the literary context of the age, an arresting novelty. The main poetic tradition, from the Troubadour verse of Provence, through Dante and Petrarch to Sidney, treated romantic love as a state apart from, or even opposed to, that of betrothal and marriage. Only in the changed, post-Reformation climate of Elizabethan England could the two kinds of experience blend. The concept of a courtship leading through romance to marriage was a major element in Spenser's interpretation

---

[2] A different time-scheme has been put forward by Alexander Dunlop, 'The Unity of Spenser's *Amoretti*', in *Silent Poetry*, ed. Alistair Fowler (1970), pp. 153–69. Dunlop believes that *Amoretti* xxii–lxviii make a group in which each sonnet corresponds to a day from Ash Wednesday (xxii) through the Lent of 1594, preceded by 21 sonnets from January 1st and followed by another 21 sonnets from Easter. But there is no necessary connection between xxii (10) and Ash Wednesday (see notes), nor any mention of Lent in the sonnets that follow. The reference to a completed year in lx (19) is quite specific. Dunlop's views are supported by O. B. Hardison Jr., '*Amoretti* and the *Dolce Stil Nuovo*', *ELH*, ii (1972), 208–16. (See Lever, 1974 edn, pp. 279–80.)

of life as evolved through the later books of *The Faerie Queene* and in the *Hymne of Love*. His Renaissance Platonism led him to view physical beauty and love as manifestations of the ideal. At the same time his Protestant creed with its stress on the virtue of marriage required that, instead of fully sublimating romance attitudes, he should seek to harmonise these with the conditions of a sanctified union based on mutual affection and respect.

The *Amoretti* sequence opens on a spiritual plane. The lady is portrayed not as a disturbing physical presence but almost as the *donna angelicata* of Dante's vision. She is a 'huge brightness', a 'light' that 'hath kindled heavenly fire' (3). Her eyes, instead of being conventionally the dwelling-place of Cupid, harbour angels who 'lead frail minds to rest / in chaste desires' (6). Not until 7—sonnet xiii in the quarto numbering—is she fully humanised, and even here she is seen as an *exemplum* of Christian virtue, walking with mingled pride and humility, her head raised to the sky, her eyes lowered to the earth. This virtue, unlike that attributed to Stella, exercises a genuine moral influence. Care is taken, however, to avoid a total sublimation. In the new year and spring sonnets love is made to accord with the rhythms and impulses of nature. The lady is a 'fair flower' (4); she should rejoice at hearing the 'merry cuckoo' (9). Yet the main trend is to assert the primacy of the moral and ideal components of love. Courtship is thus a prolonged apprenticeship to virtue, which the lover must serve with as much patience as he can summon up.

From the second new year (21) the relationship changes. The lover's suit comes to be accepted, and the tensions of courtship are eased. But Spenser's response is in marked contrast to Sidney's rapture when Stella admits to her love. It is controlled and distanced through the careful re-working of traditional images converting despair into spiritual hope, or frustration into fulfilment, as in the treatment of Petrarch's (and Wyatt's) metaphors of the ship in storm, or the fair, elusive hind (22, 24). The lady's body is frankly praised in 23, but through biblical similes and cadences that bring sexual response into an ambience of Christian symbolism.[3] Spring celebrations recur in 26, 'Fresh spring, the herald of love's mighty king'. Instead of disregarding love's

[3] See notes to this sonnet.

'precept', as in 9, the lady will now make herself ready 'to wait on Love amongst his lovely crew'. But the ancient folk paganism is balanced by the second Easter sonnet. The attraction between human beings, part of the order of nature, also corresponds on an earthly plane to God's love for man. Both Christ and the May King are lords to be obeyed.

/ Spenser's sonnets are in fact a highly original achievement. They are based on a transformation of the themes treated by Wyatt and Sidney, and the whole Petrarchan mode of courtship./The unattainable, eternally yearned for mistress of romance is won and converted into a life partner. Cupid is brought into the realm of Christian charity, with sense and spirit reconciled. The new synthesis expresses Spenser's total attitude to life. However, it is demonstrated, rather than grasped in the immediate act of composition. The *Amoretti* sequence is a limb from the main body of Spenser's work. Life and energy certainly flow through these sonnets; but they are not, as in *Astrophel and Stella*, generated from within.

Sidney's and Spenser's sequences present, in their different ways, experience transmuted into poetry. This is hardly true of the copious outpouring of sonnets in the years immediately following the first, unauthorised publication of *Astrophel and Stella* in 1591. In most of these, self-examination, emotional range, or serious exploration of the polarity of 'self' and 'other', hardly exist. The authors, parodied by Jonson in *Every Man In His Humour*, were following a fashion, and their sonnet mistresses, the Licias, Dianas, Cynthias and Fidessas, were no more than pegs on which to hang a pretty phrase or clever conceit. In so far as these sonnets had a positive aspect, it may be seen as the reflection of a diffused curiosity. Any topic of contemporary interest, from astrology to law, from witchcraft to anatomy, was drawn upon as an image or structural prop. This mechanical ingenuity was the most to be expected from such minor versifiers as Constable, Barnfield, and others. But even the sonnets of distinguished poets suggest that the old core of romance inspiration was dying. Instead these writers, notably Samuel Daniel (1562–1619) and Michael Drayton (1563–1631), turned to the perfecting of verse techniques that would convey their distinctive personal idioms.

In his power over simple words and metrical effects the most accomplished of the poets who published sonnets in the fifteen-nineties was 'well-languaged Daniel'. Twenty-seven sonnets of the 'Delia' sequence were printed together with the 1591 edition of *Astrophel and Stella*. Next year Daniel's own collection appeared, in an edition of fifty, later of fifty-two sonnets. Successive editions with changes and augmentations came out up to 1601. Choosing the verse-form of the Surrey sonnet, Daniel concentrated on effects of mood based on the conventional themes of the mistress's scorn and the lover's despair. There is little suggestion of inner conflict, but the plaintiveness and brooding melancholy of these poems gave them a distinctive quality, as did their sensitive evocation of natural beauty. Daniel had a fine ear for evocative cadences, sonorous vowel harmonies, subtle variations of metre, and the suggestion of delicacy and pathos through 'feminine' rhymes. Certain reiterated keywords—*sigh, cares, heart, glory, grieve*—with their euphonies of sound impart a sense of unity to the sequence. Within this were minor oscillations of mood. These have been seen by a recent critic as part of a conscious structural design worked out over the years.[4] They were probably suggested in the first instance by what Daniel found in his models. He drew largely on Desportes and Du Bellay, toning down hyperboles and sustaining his own gentle, plaintive manner. But in one group of sonnets, xxxi–xxxv (1–5), inspired by Ronsard and Tasso, there is a close unity of theme and structure maintained by chain-like links repeating or slightly varying the last line of a sonnet in the first line of the next. These, among the finest in the sequence, show a notable shift of concern. From the usual laments at Delia's cruelty the poet turns to reflect on the coming destruction of her beauty by time and his unique power to make her live eternally in verse. This transforms him from a humble suppliant

---

[4] C. F. Williamson, 'The Design of Daniel's *Delia*', *RES*, xix (1968), 251–60. The author finds 'a break or turning-point after Sonnet XXIV, which divides the sequence...in proportions approximating to those of the octave and sestet of a sonnet' (p. 253). This, it is thought, corresponds to a change from humility and despair to triumphant confidence in the poet's power to immortalize the lady's beauty. The difference is not, however, as marked as the argument suggests, and much depends on the tone of the French or Italian sonnets imitated. The 'dying fall' in the last numbers of *Delia* may be conventional (resembling the endings of Sidney's and Spenser's sequences), but it hardly accords with the 'octave-sestet' structure suggested for the sequence as a whole.

to the confident master of his art. Yet the art is placed at the mistress's service; Daniel does not assume the arrogant egotism of Ronsard; he needs the lady's inspiration as she needs his skill. In this reciprocal relationship a new and major theme is introduced into the Elizabethan sonnet. The pathos of self-pity is superseded by a wider awareness of change and decay, offset by faith in the creative power of the poet.

Like Daniel, Drayton brought out his sonnets in successive editions, dropping some, revising others, and adding to his sequence over many years. *Idea's Mirror* was first published in 1594; in 1599 it was enlarged and renamed *Idea*; further editions appeared up to 1619. As tradition required, the sonnets were addressed to a mistress, and in life Drayton is known to have fallen in love at an early age with his patron's daughter Anne Goodere. Nevertheless the sonnets for the most part express no romantic fervour; indeed this is explicitly disclaimed in the 1599 address to the reader: 'Into these loves who but for passion looks' (1). Instead there was a gradual development from stock hyperboles and conceits to an independent style that reflected Drayton's wide-ranging interests. His outlook is summed up in the opening line of 2, 'Like an adventurous seafarer am I', a sonnet which realistically depicts a symbolic voyage and only mentions love perfunctorily in the final couplet. Drayton's chief model was Sidney for wit and vigorous invention, though not for emotional involvement. From Sidney he learnt the art of giving freshness to an old image by setting it in a contemporary situation. 'My heart was slain' (3) offers, instead of a lament, a crime problem calling for solution; after an inquest rejecting suicide, the murderer turns out to be the boy Cupid, hiding in the mistress's eye. Sidney had shown Drayton how to use colloquial speech and wordplay instead of stilted epithets:

> I say 'I love'; you slightly answer 'Ay';
> I say 'You love'; you pule me out a 'No'. (4)

In the later sonnets Drayton develops beyond liveliness and wit towards a deeper concern with personal relationships. The easy, idiomatic tones of address come to imply a new mutuality in love: instead of idealising the mistress, the poet sees her as another human being with whom he is at once identified and distinct. Paradox serves to express tortuous involutions of selfhood:

> Give me my self, and take your self again;
> Devise some means but how I may forsake you;
> So much is mine that doth with you remain,
> That taking what is mine, with me I take you. (6)

Here Drayton approaches the intensity of Donne's appeal to God: 'Take me to you, imprison me, for I / Except you enthral me, never shall be free'. These developments come to fruition in Drayton's finest sonnet, 'Since there's no help' (14). The colloquial tone voices a profound mutual understanding behind the parting and cancellation of vows; paradox is not verbal but implicit in the situation, so that the conclusion is at once foreseeable and unexpected. In the latter part of the sonnet, with its suggestion of a Petrarchan sestet underlying the quatrain and couplet form, the death of love takes on the aspect of actual physical death, with 'faith' kneeling and 'innocence' closing up the eyes. After this, the possibility of restoration to life at the will of the beloved verges on a Christian resurrection. Drayton's last love sonnets stand at the frontier between the secular Renaissance tradition and the devotional ambience of the metaphysical poets.

Great poetry cannot be understood in terms of 'sources'' 'influences', or 'trends'. Shakespeare's sonnets have their affinities with those of other poets in the 1590s, but nothing in the work of his contemporaries, even Daniel and Drayton, would have led anyone to foresee their appearance. In an age when the romance tradition was dying out and poets were seeking new themes to reflect a changing world, these sonnets recreate the old values in a timeless perspective. No summary account can begin to do justice to them. After many admirable interpretations, exploration must be constantly renewed.

Shakespeare's *Sonnets* were first published in 1609. Like the first editions of *Astrophel and Stella* and *Amoretti*, the quarto seems to have been unauthorised, without preface or dedication by the poet or any mention by him of when the sonnets were composed or to whom they were addressed. Thomas Thorpe's florid dedication 'To the only begetter of these ensuing sonnets Mr. W.H.', is highly ambiguous; these common initials might signify the person who inspired the poems, or whoever procured them for publication, or even the poet under some pseudonym or nickname. Resemblances in style, imagery and phrasing link many sonnets with Shakespeare's writing in the 1590s, and some were already known by 1598.[5] The order may be questionable in detail, but the main groupings are fairly clear: (1) a long series of 126 sonnets to a young man, rounded off by an *envoi* in couplets; (2) a short series of 26 sonnets centred upon an affair with a mistress; (3) two occasional sonnets, inferior in style, working out stock erotic conceits. Questions about the historical identity of the young man, the mistress, the rival poets mentioned in the long series, or the name behind the initials 'W.H.', remain unanswered. Like other Renaissance sonnet-writers, Shakespeare was not primarily concerned with individualisation. The relationship, not the actual person, was all-important.

The first series is not only much longer, but far more complex than the second. It opens with seventeen sonnets amounting to a carefully argued plea for the young man to marry and beget an heir. Arguments from Erasmus and Sidney's *Arcadia* are linked with Shakespeare's own deep preoccupations with the decay of beauty, the tyranny of time, and the uniqueness of personality. Towards the end of the group the argument shifts, at first hesitantly, then with growing confidence, to an affirmation that the friend will be given eternal life in verse. Through the rest of the series, in spite of absences, estrangements, rivalries, lapse of time and change of circumstances, the poet's faith in his power to immortalise the friend is constantly declared. His ability proceeds only from his love; or rather, from an act of creation wholly identified with his love, which transcends time and mutability. It is verified by the poetry itself:

> If this be error, and upon me proved,
> I never writ, nor no man ever loved. (39)

The nature of this love is unique in the history of the sonnet; not because it is directed towards a young man instead of a mistress, but because it looks to no consummation. Homosexual desire, like heterosexual, aims at a fulfilment. Even when sublimated into a Platonic pursuit of the 'ideal', it seeks possession of the self that is idealised. Shakespeare's concerns, even from the start of the series, lie elsewhere. In his plea for marriage and offspring, Shakespeare states the rationale of such a courtship

[5] Francis Meres in *Palladis Tamia* (1598) referred to Shakespeare's 'sugred sonnets among his private friends'.

as Spenser's in the *Amoretti*; yet there is no personal involvement.
All that matters is that through procreation the friend's beauty
and truth should be rescued from time. Whereas Spenser had
welcomed time into his courtship as a necessary process of fruition,
Shakespeare challenges it as the foe to all that is loveable in life—
summer, the 'darling buds of May', 'everything that grows'. Of
this 'everything' the friend is the essence and epitome; his end
will be 'truth's and beauty's doom and date'. It is a love which,
far from being possessive or exclusive, comprehends in the
beloved all that stirs the creative imagination in the phenomenal
world. Like every form of creativeness, it is charged with sexual
energy; but the sexuality is not particularised. 'It is as though
Shakespeare could only apprehend the meaningfulness of life
when it was, for him, incarnated in a person, and as though
he could only love a person as the incarnation of that meaning-
fulness.'[6]

The series may thus be said to rest on a major antinomy, be-
tween the forces of cosmic negation summed up in the 'forty
winters' (1), which lay siege to beauty, and the friend's 'eternal
summer' (9) miraculously reclaimed in the 'eternal lines' of
verse. Through successive sonnets time's works are presented
with mounting complexity. Ovid's classic survey of mutability
in the last book of the *Metamorphoses* is restated together with
Shakespeare's own perceptions. The interchange of sea and land,
the rise and fall of kings, eclipses of sun and moon, the growth
and decay of men and plants alike, coalesce through many
permutations in a vision of universal flux. In counterpoise, the
love of the friend is affirmed on every level of perception as a
work of creative redemption accomplished through the poetry
it generates.

By this antinomy the sonnets take into their scope the age's
preoccupation with mobility and change, together with its
elevation of creative art as a transcendence of nature. The miracle
of art, however, which restores a paradisal eternal summer, is
wrought through human love. Accordingly the series to the
friend also partakes of the Petrarchan vision. Whatever the
friend amounts to as an imaginative construct, he remains a
person loved by a person. The experience of the sonnets includes
the traditional themes of absence, misunderstanding, reproach,

[6] J. B. Leishman, *Themes and Variations in Shakespeare's Sonnets* (1961), p. 51.

solitude, jealousy. All these topics are present, yet all are subtly re-shaped. Sidney had prayed that in dreams he might 'Stella see': that the mind in sleep might offer a substitute for the object of desire. Shakespeare views his friend in darkness, though awake with open eyes, through his 'soul's imaginary sight' (12). It is not the friend's favour that brings the poet to 'heaven's gate', but the very act of imagining: 'Haply I *think* on thee' (13). The rivals are not sexual lovers but other poets, and the main danger from them is the distortion of the friend's image through false art. The transformation is complete in 39, where the Petrarchan metaphor of love as the tempest that wrecks the lover's bark becomes an image of love as 'an ever-fixèd mark / That looks on tempests and is never shaken'. The vicissitudes of romance find their resolution in a secular religion where poetry is prayer, imagination is faith, and human love the universal redeemer.

The shorter series to the mistress makes up a kind of confused anti-masque to the series to the friend. Here elegant conceits mingle with bitter invective, scepticism with spiritual conflict, obscene innuendoes with agonised reproach. Irony is the keynote; sometimes poised and outwardly directed; sometimes involuted and self-wounding. These sonnets present the opposite face to the affirmations of the main series. Instead of a love whose sexuality is merged in the poet's outgoing concern with every aspect of life, love is obsessively fixed upon a single object of desire. As for the mistress herself, she is, like the friend, what the poet chooses to make her. The infatuation need not have seemed very different from any other in the romance tradition: egotistic, oblivious of a world beyond itself, ultimately bringing conscience and desire into collision. It becomes more sinister and more daemonic through its place in a wider poetic setting.

In terms of 'story' the minor series is linked to the major through the involvement of the friend in the intrigue. But its special quality need not be narrowed down to this triangular complication, whatever it signified in life. The very nature of the erotic experience forms a necessary complement to that of the major series. All the positive aspects of romance had been taken up into the friendship with the young man. Instead the affair with the mistress reaches down to a hidden polarity where sexual being functions as a blind, impersonal urge. Up to a point this brings a sense of release. The lark tires of singing at heaven's gate; there is an earthing of poetic energy. In praising the mistress, romance sublimation is parodied and sexual desire uncovered through graceful and witty conceits. These lead on to more sweeping ironies. Beauty and truth are themselves negated, and pleasure found in the recognition that because the lover and mistress lie *to* each other they are free to lie *with* each other (51). 'Conscience' is taken in the amoral sense of 'knowing', or carnal knowledge; with priapic humour its physical workings are described. Sonnets of wordplay on 'Will'—as name, as synonym for lust, as the auxiliary to verbs of pure action—strip away personality and its ideal pretensions. The nihilistic descent is, perhaps, necessary to creative functioning. With Lawrence, Shakespeare could say:

> I have been, and I have returned.
> I have mounted up on the wings of the morning, and I
> have dredged down to the zenith's reversal.
> Which is my way, being man.   (*Saint Matthew*)

But the descent too must reach a nadir. Service to Priapus brings its own slavery, and generates a desperate struggle between reason and desire. In other sonnets love is a 'blind fool' who deceives the eyes and through them the heart (50). It is a fever perverting the appetite, so that the patient disobeys the physician Reason, who leaves him to his madness (54). Ultimately the conflict is seen in terms of Christian dualities; heaven-hell, angel-fiend. The draining of sexual energy in coition is equated to 'The expense of spirit in a waste of shame' (47). Here Shakespeare looks back to Sidney's 'Leave me, O love', and forward to Donne's *Divine Sonnets*. The body, foredoomed to perish, must be starved to save the soul, which in return will feed on death. Love's fulfilment cannot be known in the flesh.

Northrop Frye has written of Shakespeare's sonnets: 'They are a poetic realization of the whole range of love in the western world, from the idealism of Petrarch to the ironic frustrations of Proust'.[7] Yet this vast range of experience is organised through the basically simple verse form of the Tudor sonnet, with its logic of apposition, contrast, and inferential conclusion. Most typically the thought is developed through three strongly marked units of syntax, shaped by the quatrains, often introduced by the

[7] Northrop Frye, in *The Riddle of Shakespeare's Sonnets*, ed. Edward Hubler (1962), p. 53.

keywords '*When...When...When...*', or '*When...Then...Then...*', leading to a summation in the couplet, '*And yet*'. Sometimes inner complexities arise; the thought may become agitated, building up extra tension in the third quatrain, or packing the tension into the first eight lines, to find release on a different plane of thought in the rest of the sonnet. Here the Petrarchan structure of octave-sestet reasserts itself through the English quatrains; yet even so the essential process is that of inferential reasoning. This may proceed without verbal connections, each stage of logic depending on the previous one like uncemented stone blocks resting on their own weight. It may be woven into the texture of a conceit. Or uniquely in 47, one property, lust, may be denounced in all its implications and effects through twelve lines of unhalted invective, the logical inference being withheld until the final couplet.

In use of words as in verse form the sonnets keep up the Tudor preference for simplicity. In the earlier poems of the 'friend' series Shakespeare matches and surpasses Daniel in melodious long vowels and cadences: 'Beauty o'ersnowed, and bareness everywhere', 'When to the sessions of sweet silent thought'. But increasingly this smooth patterning gives way to a plainer diction modelled upon the spoken word: 'Alas, tis true', 'Might I not then say, "Now I love you best" ', 'I grant I never saw a goddess go'. This is controlled by the standard rhythm of the pentameter with its regular alternating stresses. Only when special striking effects are called for do alliteration and assonance become obtrusive—'Ruin hath taught me thus to ruminate'—or stresses irregular—'Love is not love', 'Savage, extreme, rude, cruel, not to trust'.

Imagery functions on many levels. There are similes which spring from deep roots in Shakespeare's creative response and recur frequently in his writing: the lark at break of day, the jewel seen at night. At the other extreme, conceits and wordplay may serve to pinpoint a single occasion. In the series to the friend the imagery has some affinities to both Daniel's and Drayton's; but Shakespeare's perceptions of nature are not merely decorative or pathetic, nor are his everyday allusions only there for their topicality. Both kinds are related to universal themes—time's cruel hand, the lease of life, death's arrest. Characteristically they tend to be fused in compound metaphors that integrate different aspects of reality—seasonal change, political conflict, human beauty and vulnerability. Certain motifs recur and are blended together: Sun, Rose, King, Sea, as paragons of beauty or virtue, grace or power, in the phenomenal world, are set against Time in its various manifestations. These may be drawn into a kind of continuum, as in 23, lines 5–8. Similarly the imaginative truth of love may be presented through other fused images of transcendence—child, edifice, plant, as in 43.[8]

Beneath all this complexity, which strains articulation to the limit, lies the uniqueness of the poetic force that Shakespeare identifies with love. It reaches out in every direction to grapple with time, mutability, and death. Yet so pure is it in essence that it functions most typically through the simple logic-patterns of the English sonnet form, the plainest words, the most familiar images. Even in the mistress series, descending into a chaos that obliterates objects and ideas, the same thought-processes are still at work with indestructible clarity and objectivity.

Shakespeare carried to its limits the power of the sonnet to explore human love in the phenomenal world. For other writers in the late fifteen-nineties the theme was exhausted. Increasingly they turned towards metaphysical enquiry and cosmological speculations. Thought became more abstract and austere. Instead of dwelling on the plight of a beloved person subject to age and mutability, poets chose to grapple with the paradoxes of time and eternity, essence and existence. Such reasoning, itself impassioned, also took on a more personal cast, in a heightened concern for the spiritual predicament of the individual. A religious polarity, of the soul in its relation to God, came to replace the romance polarity of lover and beloved. This was to transform the primary theme of the sonnet, which moved from the contrarieties of sexual love to those of Christian doctrine and faith. In essence the change reflected the new religious individualism, the turn to meditation and self-searching, which spread through Europe in the later sixteenth century. In poetry it found expression through a transposition of familiar sonnet topics. 'Deprivation of the unkind or absent mistress becomes deprivation of God's grace. The mistress had been an absolute, an ideal, an unchangeable, as contrasted to the flawed, fallen,

[8] See notes to these sonnets.

and changeable particulars of creation: so is God'.[9] Accordingly old sonnet motifs appeared in a changed guise. Instead of wearing the portrait of the mistress or friend in his bosom, the spiritual lover found there the image of Christ. Instead of freezing in his lady's disdain, he saw his heart as a frozen desert unmelted by the beams of the divine sun—or Son. Night brought, not disturbing dreams of the beloved, but turbulent thoughts of death and damnation. At the same time a new stream of images entered the sonnet from biblical and doctrinal sources. Paradise and the Fall, crucifixion and resurrection, were taken as correspondences to the vicissitudes of the soul. Here, too, inherent dilemmas were revealed to the questioning mind. Contradiction and paradox, the conflicts of reason and faith, were built into the new sonnet structure as into the old.

The *Caelica* sequence of Fulke Greville, Lord Brooke (1554–1628) marks the transition from the romance to the metaphysical mode. Greville's subtle, enquiring mind ranged widely over the major issues of the age; in his unprinted dramas *Mustapha* and *Alaham* he would question the foundations of church and state; at the same time he was keenly aware of the sterility of reason without faith. *Caelica* has the form of the traditional love sequence, but, as its title ('heavenly one') suggests, the lady is rather a concept than a person. After some earlier sonnets, light or playful exercises in a fashionable medium, Greville turned to more abstruse reflections. Caelica's rejection of the poet and availability to other men are expressed in conceits describing her heart as a lost paradise or tower of Babel, with knowledge and divine justice as the poet's enemies, frustrating his quest for heavenly peace (1, 2). Evidently the real theme lies in the religious allusions, disguised by the erotic complaint which is the ostensible subject of the sonnet. Through the mask of the fickle mistress Greville perceives a deity from whom he is alienated; though others, paradoxically—the very builders of 'Babel'—are accepted. In yet later sonnets the topic of the mistress is given up and the poet's inner conflicts or doubts are dwelt on for their own sake. Night is dissociated from thoughts of love and made the occasion for reflection on the working of the mind when external illumination is lost (4). The sonnet maintains a troubled ambiguity: is the fear stirred up by 'witty tyranny' with its 'news of

[9] *Selected Poems of Fulke Greville*, ed. Thom Gunn (1968), p. 35.

devils' a psychological delusion, or the soul's foreshadowing of real devils that await it in 'thick depriving darknesses'? In 'Love is the peace whereto all thought doth strive' (3) Greville achieves perfect poise through compressed, unadorned statement. Love, 'Passed through hope, desire, grief and fear' is 'A simple goodness in the flesh refined'. Yet in the context of the sequence, this resolution seems rather wished for than attained. It must be set against the castigation of 'false and treacherous probability' (5), where the operations of reason are denounced with self-wounding fervour and the poem ends by denying any possibility that 'inward bliss' may be found in the world of time. These sonnets with their spare diction, avoidance of any but the most functional images, and simple Surrey quatrains, are masterly products of the plain style.

Another poet who took the conventional sequence as a framework for speculation was William Drummond of Hawthornden (1585–1649). A Scottish country gentleman living on his estate, Drummond was somewhat isolated from changing currents of taste. His sonnets, published in 1621 and 1630, are in the late-Elizabethan mode, strongly influenced by the sixteenth-century European tradition and especially by Sidney. Yet though the subjects and often the expressions are derivative, their tone of still contemplation, gentle melancholy and piety is Drummond's own. Thus in 'How that vast heaven entitled First' (1) the structure recalls *Astrophel and Stella* 14, but the questions raised are cosmic and universal, not political and immediate, while the allusion to love in the couplet seems perfunctory. Platonic notions of the soul's pre-existence, reflections on life as a 'passing glance', a 'spark' struck by 'contraries' (5), and on the mind's transcendence of 'the floating world' (6) are characteristic of Drummond's 'wandering thoughts'. Renaissance idealism and Christian faith blend harmoniously to fortify a temperament that seeks calm retreat from mutability. Drummond's smooth, plangent adaptations of Sidney's sonnet form are in keeping with his capacity for surveying the intellectual and spiritual turmoil of the age with sad but quiet detachment.

In sharp contrast, the sonnets of William Alabaster (1567–1640) are a product of intense involvement. These poems were composed in the months of 1597–98 when Alabaster, then a Fellow of Trinity, Cambridge, became a convert to Roman

Catholicism. The decision meant a break with beloved relatives and friends, the end of a secure, scholarly career, and the imminent threat of imprisonment as a recusant. In the 'Personal Sonnets' Alabaster voiced at once elation in his faith and pain at the wrenching of every familiar tie. From Sidney's sonnets to Stella he took the idiomatic tone and flexible speech-rhythms:

> This is the bill: dearness, affection,
> Friends, fortune, pleasure, fame, hope, life undone,
> Want, prison, torment, death, shame—what behind? (1)

But with this went a vehemence and fervour sprung from a different kind of dedication: not to courtly love, but to the service of Christ. Sidney's infatuation had bred doubts and moral conflicts; Alabaster's opened up the prospect of martyrdom and called for a virtual renunciation of his old personality. Such issues could not be expressed through the traditional romance motifs. Alabaster turned, like his French near-contemporary La Ceppède, to the set meditation as a source of sonnet motifs. The exercise called for a fixing of the mind upon some theme from the gospel or other high mystery. *Divine Meditations* centre round the events of the crucifixion and resurrection, perceived as analogues to the poet's spiritual trials. The attempt to identify with Christ vividly lit up his own failings and the disparity between mental resolution and emotional wavering—'Heaven of my mind...Death of my heart' (10), leading to sudden shifts of tone and striking conceits. 'Though all forsake thee, Lord' (5) suggests through the octave a supremely confident affirmation of faith; in the sestet the impression is shattered as the pledge is seen to be an echoing of St. Peter's promise to Christ, broken at the first test. Alabaster wrote with prescience: in life his fervour would soon cool and he would find his way back to the less exacting ways of the Anglicanism in which he had been bred. Yet this emotional instability, yoked with an intellect of much acuteness and capacity for self-knowledge, generates the poetic energy of the sonnets. In the main these show an easy command of form, with a flexible use of Italian, French, and Sidneian rhyme-schemes. More important than technical facility is the rhetorical drive, imaginative treatment of functional conceits—as in the working out of the thorn and rose symbolism in 7—and precision of thought, which in the octave of 8 produces a memorable synthesis of the concepts of time and eternity. Almost unknown until they were edited in 1959, these sonnets stand out as the first expressions of devotional verse in the metaphysical mode.

While Alabaster's poems reflect a single brief phrase of spiritual crisis, Donne's were composed over many years of complex growth. As a man, moreover, Donne's range of sensibilities was far wider and his thought more intricate. The *Holy Sonnets*, written in 1609, cannot be dissociated from the secular love poems and prose composition of his middle years. They carry over to a spiritual plane the same intellectual curiosity and strong sensuous response, together with a characteristic impatience with prescribed attitudes. Two years earlier Donne had composed *La Corona*, a set of thirteen devotional sonnets based on the themes of the Rosary, where, as in a group in Daniel's *Delia*, the last line of each sonnet was repeated in the first line of the next. But the strict patterning of thought had cramped his poetic powers, and in the new series he gave himself more creative scope. While the set meditation underlies some of the *Holy Sonnets*, it supplies inspiration rather than a formula. In 'At the round earth's imagined corners' (4) his imagination is fired by the subject of the Day of Judgement; his thoughts are set racing by the magnificent spectacle and wonder of resurrection, and an intensely dramatic *mise-en-scène* results. But in the excitement the purpose of meditation—the inducing of a mood of devout self-surrender —is forgotten through the octave, and when Donne returns to his own predicament he must call on God, as if he were addressing the stage-manager, to halt the production and give him time to repent. Contrition is present from the start in 'Spit in my face, ye Jews' (7); but only to over-reach itself. Instead of identifying himself, as piety required, with the humiliated Christ, he puts himself in the place of the Jews; indeed he is worse than these; for while they merely 'killed once an inglorious man', he daily crucifies Christ glorified. An excessively alert mind has produced the doctrinally awkward claim that today's ordinary Christian sinner is more culpable than the 'impious Jews' of gospel times. The restless play of thought in these sonnets make them unique as devotional poems, if doubtful exemplars of religious rectitude.

The first six of the *Holy Sonnets* are a consideration of the Augustinian Four Last Things—Death, Judgement, Hell, and Heaven. With their free-wheeling approach and lively analogies

from secular life they come closer to Sir Thomas More's treatise
on the subject than to the schematic reasoning of theologians.
Generally Donne wears his devoutness with a difference. An
earnest craving for grace and pardon alternates with impetuous
questionings, strange convolutions of thought, and intrusions
of the irrepressible, unregenerate self. In the first sonnet, a
preparatory prayer, the poet wants to know why Satan has more
power over his soul than God, and admonishes the deity for not
enforcing his rights. 'If poisonous minerals' (5), reviewing the
prospect of hell, opens not with a confession of sin, but a protest
at the divine policy of damning man, alone of all creatures, for
the faculty of reason with which God had endowed him. The
sestet indeed recoils from this dangerous position; but instead of
turning to hopes of grace, it voices passionate despair and pleads
only for oblivion. Moving from hell to thoughts of heaven, 'Death
be not proud' (6) swings back to unqualified confidence in salva-
tion. The force of the poem lies not in the sophistry that transfers
the mishaps of man's life to a personified Death, but in the
irregular surges of rhythm conveying a precarious elation.

A second group of six sonnets centres first on God's love for
man, then on man's love for God; the construction, however, is
not closely knit. 'Spit in my face' (7), with its heterodox implica-
tions, is followed by the more conventional meditation 'Why are
we by all creatures' (8), which makes amends for the complaints
of 5; but the following sonnets stray into romance conceits that
seem incongruous in their spiritual context. Donne's compliments
to the 'beauteous form' of his 'profane mistresses' are hardly
relevant to the picturing of Christ in his agony (9); nor is the
identification of beauty with goodness, ugliness with evil, a truly
Christian line of reasoning. Similarly in 10 the image of the soul
as a besieged fortress changes into an incongruous situation, where
the poet becomes a girl in distress who disturbingly begs to be
ravished by her lover rather than married to his enemy. Four
penitential sonnets, later incorporated with the original twelve,
give up the meditational approach for direct expressions of
contrition. The note of piety is strongly sustained, but intellectual
tension is lost and the poems tend to become fourteen-line
monologues without clearly functioning verse units. Three other
sonnets which remained in manuscript till 1899 (11, 12) are at
once more revealing and more formally effective. 'Since she

whom I loved' (13) alludes to Donne's dead wife. Earthly love has now been replaced by heavenly thoughts; why then is God still inclined to 'tender jealousy'? Through the reproach an undercurrent of uneasiness at Donne's own professions of spirituality can be felt. Scepticism about the rival claims of the various churches in 14 leads, as in 10, to romance conceits and an intrusive sexuality. In the final sonnet (15) comes a full admission of chronic instability. As with Shakespeare's love of the mistress, religion for Donne is a fever: his 'devout fits come and go away / Like a fantastic ague'.

In form Donne's sonnets follow Sidney's; both reflect the conflicts of reason and emotion, affirmation and doubt, through the duality of octave and sestet, often with a paradoxical conclusion hammered home by the couplet. In a wider sense, they belong to the essential tradition of the English sonnet from the first experiments of Wyatt. Whatever the chosen theme—friendship, romance, sacramental marriage, or the soul's search for unity with God—a substratum of tough, knotty individualism prevails. Conventions are respected, whether sprung from the code of courtly love or from the doctrines of Christianity; but they are pragmatically interpreted and, where necessary, transformed.

Without the romance vision of Italian and French verse, where the imagination ranged from a base of intellectual acceptance, the English poets proceeded through a constant awareness of doubt and contradiction, alternating between precarious self-assertion and deliberate self-effacement, but always maintaining a distinctive stance. In our own time, when poetry has become synonymous with self-expression and established forms are suspect, the sonnets of the English Renaissance may at first sight appear over-concerned with conventional attitudes and modes of expression. A better understanding of their idioms and the functioning of their verse technique may reveal an insight into the timeless workings of personality as complex and revealing as most lyrical creations of a later age.

BIBLIOGRAPHY

Note. Short form references as used in the introduction and notes
are shown on the left.

Bateson	F. W. Bateson, *English Poetry: A Critical Introduction* (1950)
Booth	Stephen Booth, *An Essay on Shakespeare's Sonnets* (1969)
Bullough	*The Poetry and Plays of Fulke Greville, First Lord Brooke,* ed. Geoffrey Bullough (1939)
Dover Wilson	*The Sonnets,* The New Shakespeare, ed. John Dover Wilson (1966)
Gardner	*John Donne, 'The Divine Poems',* ed. Helen Gardner (1952)
Gunn	*Selected Poems of Fulke Greville,* ed. Thom Gunn (1968)
Hebel	*The Works of Michael Drayton,* ed. J. W. Hebel (1931–1941, 1961), vols. i. ii
Hotson	Leslie Hotson, *Shakespeare's Sonnets Dated* (1949)
Ingram and Redpath	*Shakespeare's Sonnets,* ed. W. Ingram and T. Redpath (1964)
John	Lisle Cecil John, *The Elizabethan Sonnet Sequences: Studies in Conventional Conceits* (1938)
Jones	*The Poems of Henry Howard, Earl of Surrey,* ed. Emrys Jones (1966)
Kalstone	David Kalstone, *Sidney's Poetry: Contexts and Interpretations* (1965)
Kastner	*The Poetical Works of William Drummond of Hawthornden,* ed. L. E. Kastner (1913, 1968)
Lever	J. W. Lever, *The Elizabethan Love Sonnet* (1956, 1966, 1974)
Mahood	Molly M. Mahood, *Shakespeare's Wordplay* (1957)
Martz (1)	Louis L. Martz, *The Poetry of Meditation* (1954, 1962)
Martz (2)	'The Action of the Self: Devotional Poetry in the Seventeenth Century', *Stratford-upon-Avon Studies* 11 (1970)
Mizener	Arthur Mizener, 'The Structure of Figurative Language in Shakespeare's Sonnets', *Southern Review,* v (1940). Reprinted in *Discussions of Shakespeare's Sonnets,* ed. Barbara Herrnstein (1964)

Muir (1)   *Collected Poems of Sir Thomas Wyatt*, ed. Kenneth Muir
                    (1949)
Muir (2)   Kenneth Muir, *Sir Philip Sidney* (1960)
Ransom   John Crowe Ransom, 'Shakespeare At Sonnets',
                    Southern Review, iv (1938). Reprinted in *Discussions of
                    Shakespeare's Sonnets* (see Mizener)
RES   *Review of English Studies*
Ringler   *The Poems of Sir Philip Sidney*, ed. William A. Ringler
                    (1962)
Schaar (1)   Claes Schaar, *Elizabethan Sonnet Themes and the Dating of
                    Shakespeare's Sonnets* (1962)
Schaar (2)   'A Textual Puzzle in Daniel's *Delia*', *English Studies*, xl
                    (1959)
Sprague   Samuel Daniel, *'Poems' and 'A Defence of Rhyme'*, ed.
                    Arthur Colby Sprague (1930, 1950)
Story and   *The Sonnets of William Alabaster*, ed. G. M. Story and
  Gardner   Helen Gardner (1959)
Thomson (1)   Patricia Thomson, *Sir Thomas Wyatt and His Background*
                    (1964)
Thomson (2)   'Wyatt and the Petrarchan Commentators', *Review of
                    English Studies*, x (1959)
Wilson, Mona   *Sir Philip Sidney, 'Astrophel and Stella'*, ed. Mona Wilson
                    (1931)
Wilson, Thomas   Thomas Wilson, *The Art of Rhetoric* (1553)

AS   *Astrophel and Stella*
Amor.   *Amoretti*
ShS   *Shakespeare's Sonnets*
HS   *Holy Sonnets* (Donne)

SIR THOMAS WYATT (1503-42)

1

Whoso list to hunt, I know where is an hind,
  But as for me, helas, I may no more;
  The vain travail hath wearied me so sore,
  I am of them that farthest come behind.
Yet may I by no means my wearied mind
  Draw from the Deer; but as she fleeth afore,
  Fainting I follow; I leave off therefore,
  Since in a net I seek to hold the wind.
Who list her hunt, I put him out of doubt,
  As well as I may spend his time in vain;
  And, graven in diamonds, in letters plain
There is written her fair neck round about:
  '*Noli me tangere*, for Caesar's I am;
  And wildè for to hold, though I seem tame'.

2

My galley, chargèd with forgetfulness,
  Thorough sharp seas in winter nights doth pass
  'Tween rock and rock, and eke mine enemy, alas,
  That is my Lord, steereth with cruelness;
And every oar a thought in readiness,
  As though that death were light in such a case.
  An endless wind doth tear the sail apace,
  Of forcèd sighs and trusty fearfulness.
A rain of tears, a cloud of dark disdain,
  Hath done the wearèd cords great hinderance,
  Wreathed with error and eke with ignorance.
The stars be hid that led me to this pain;
  Drownèd is reason that should me consort,
  And I remain despairing of the port.

3

You that in love find luck and abundance
   And live in lust and joyful jollity,
   Arise for shame! Do away your sluggardy!
   Arise, I say, do May some observance!
Let me in bed lie dreaming in mischance;
   Let me remember the haps most unhappy
   That me betide in May most commonly,
   As one whom love list little to advance.
Sephame said true that my nativity
   Mischanced was with the ruler of the May:
   He guessed, I prove, of that the verity.
In May my wealth and eke my life, I say,
   Have stond so oft in such perplexity.
   Rejoice! Let me dream of your felicity.

4

To rail or jest ye know I use it not,
   Though that such cause sometime in folks I find;
   And though to change ye list to set your mind,
   Love it who list, in faith I like it not.
And if ye were to me as ye are not,
   I would be loath to see you so unkind;
   But since your faith must needs be so, be kind:
   Though I hate it, I pray you love it not.
Things of great weight I never thought to crave:
   This is but small; of right deny it not.
   Your faining ways as yet forget them not,
But like reward let other lovers have:
   That is to say, for service true and fast,
   Too long delays, and changing at the last.

5

Divers doth use, as I have heard and know,
   When that to change their ladies do begin,
   To mourn and wail, and never for to lin,
   Hoping thereby to pease their painful woe.
And some there be, that when it chanceth so
   That women change, and hate where love hath been,
   They call them false, and think with words to win
   The hearts of them which otherwhere doth grow.
But as for me, though that by chance indeed
   Change hath outworn the favour that I had,
   I will not wail, lament, nor yet be sad;
Nor call her false that falsely did me feed:
   But let it pass, and think it is of kind
   That often change doth please a woman's mind.

6

The pillar perished is whereto I lent,
   The strongest stay of mine unquiet mind;
   The like of it no man again can find
   From east to west, still seeking though he went.
To mine unhap! For hap away hath rent
   Of all my joy the very bark and rind;
   And I, alas, by chance am thus assigned
   Dearly to mourn till death do it relent.
But since that thus it is by destiny,
   What can I more but have a woeful heart,
   My pen in plaint, my voice in careful cry,
My mind in woe, my body full of smart,
   And I myself myself always to hate,
   Till dreadful death do ease my doleful state?

HENRY HOWARD, EARL OF SURREY
(1517?–47)

I

Love that doth reign and live within my thought,
And built his seat within my captive breast,
Clad in the arms wherein with me he fought
Oft in my face he doth his banner rest.
But she that taught me love and suffer pain,
My doubtful hope and eke my hot desire,
With shamefast look to shadow and refrain,
Her smiling grace converteth straight to ire.
And coward Love then to the heart apace
Taketh his flight, where he doth lurk and plain,
His purpose lost, and dare not show his face.
For my lord's guilt thus faultless bide I pain;
    Yet from my lord shall not my foot remove:
    Sweet is the death that taketh end by love.

2

Divers thy death do diversely bemoan.
Some that in presence of that lively head
Lurked, whose breasts envy with hate had sown,
Yield Caesar's tears upon Pompeius' head.
Some that watchèd with the murderer's knife,
With eager thirst to drink thy guiltless blood,
Whose practice brake by happy end of life,
Weep envious tears to hear thy fame so good.
But I, that know what harboured in that head,
What virtues rare were tempered in that breast,
Honour the place that such a jewel bred,
And kiss the ground whereas thy corse doth rest
    With vapoured eyes, from whence such streams avail
    As Pyramus did on Thisbe's breast bewail.

3

The Assyrians' king, in peace with foul desire
And filthy lust that stained his regal heart,
In war that should set princely hearts afire
Vanquished did yield, for want of martial art.
The dent of swords from kisses seemèd strange,
And harder than his lady's side his targe;
From glutton feasts to soldier's fare a change,
His helmet far above a garland's charge.
Who scarce the name of manhood did retain,
Drenchèd in sloth and womanish delight,
Feeble of sprite, unpatient of pain,
When he had lost his honour and his right,
 Proud, time of wealth, in storms appalled with dread,
 Murdered himself to show some manly deed.

4

Norfolk sprang thee, Lambeth holds thee dead,
Clere, of the county of Cleremont though hight;
Within the womb of Ormonde's race thou bred,
And sawest thy cousin crownèd in thy sight.
Shelton for love, Surrey for lord thou chase;
Ay me, while life did last that league was tender!
Tracing whose steps thou sawest Kelsall blaze,
Landrecy burnt, and battered Boulogne render.
At Montreuil gates, hopeless of all recure,
Thine earl, half dead, gave in thy hand his will;
Which cause did thee this pining death procure
Ere summers four times seven thou couldst fulfil.
 Ah Clere, if love had booted, care, or cost,
 Heaven had not won, nor earth so timely lost.

SIR PHILIP SIDNEY (1554–86)

Astrophel and Stella

1 (I)

Loving in truth, and fain in verse my love to show,
    That she, dear she, might take some pleasure of my pain;
    Pleasure might cause her read, reading might make her know,
    Knowledge might pity win, and pity grace obtain,
I sought fit words to paint the blackest face of woe,
    Studying inventions fine her wits to entertain;
    Oft turning others' leaves, to see if thence would flow
    Some fresh and fruitful showers upon my sunburned brain.
But words came halting forth, wanting Invention's stay,
    Invention, Nature's child, fled stepdame Study's blows,
    And others' feet still seemed but strangers in my way.
Thus great with child to speak, and helpless in my throes,
    Biting my truant pen, beating myself for spite,
    'Fool,' said my Muse to me, 'look in thy heart and write'.

2 (II)

Not at first sight, nor with a dribbèd shot
    Love gave the wound, which while I breathe will bleed:
    But known worth did in mine of time proceed,
    Till by degrees it had full conquest got.
I saw and liked; I liked, but lovèd not;
    I loved, but straight did not what Love decreed;
    At length to Love's decrees I, forced, agreed,
    Yet with repining at so partial lot.
Now even that footstep of lost liberty
    Is gone, and now, like slave-born Muscovite,
    I call it praise to suffer tyranny;
And now employ the remnant of my wit
    To make myself believe that all is well,
    While with a feeling skill I paint my hell.

3 (III)

Let dainty wits cry on the Sisters Nine
   That, bravely masked, their fancies may be told;
   Or, Pindar's apes, flaunt they in phrases fine,
   Enamelling with pied flowers their thoughts of gold;
Or else let them in statelier glory shine,
   Ennobling new-found tropes with problems old;
   Or with strange similes enrich each line
   Of herbs or beasts which Ind or Afric hold.
For me, in sooth, no muse but one I know;
   Phrases and problems from my reach do grow,
   And strange things cost too dear for my poor sprites.
How then? Even thus: in Stella's face I read
   What love and beauty be; then all my deed
   But copying is what in her Nature writes.

4 (V)

It is most true that eyes are formed to serve
   The inward light, and that the heavenly part
   Ought to be king; from whose rules who do swerve,
   Rebels to nature, strive for their own smart.
It is most true, what we call Cupid's dart
   An image is, which for ourselves we carve,
   And, fools, adore in temple of our heart,
   Till that good god make church and churchman starve.
True, that true beauty virtue is indeed,
   Whereof this beauty can be but a shade
   Which elements with mortal mixture breed;
True, that on earth we are but pilgrims made,
   And should in soul up to our country move:
   True, and yet true that I must Stella love.

5 (VIII)

Love, born in Greece, of late fled from his native place,
   Forced by a tedious proof that Turkish hardened heart
   Is no fit mark to pierce with his fine pointed dart,
   And pleased with our soft peace, stayed here his flying
     race.
But finding these north climes do coldly him embrace,
   Not used to frozen clips, he strave to find some part
   Where with most ease and warmth he might employ his
     art;
   At length he perched himself in Stella's joyful face.
Whose fair skin, beamy eyes, like morning sun on snow,
   Deceived the quaking boy, who thought from so pure light
   Effects of lively heat must needs in nature grow.
But she, most fair, most cold, made him thence take his
     flight
   To my close heart, where, while some firebrands he did
     lay,
   He burnt unwares his wings, and cannot fly away.

6 (X)

Reason, in faith thou art well served, that still
   Wouldst brabbling be with Sense and Love in me:
   I rather wished thee climb the Muses' hill,
   Or reach the fruit of Nature's choicest tree,
Or seek heaven's course, or heaven's inside to see:
   Why shouldst thou toil our thorny soil to till?
   Leave Sense, and those who Sense's objects be;
   Deal thou with powers of thoughts, leave Love to will.
But thou wouldst needs fight both with Love and Sense,
   With sword of wit giving wounds of dispraise,
   Till downright blows did foil thy cunning fence:
For, soon as they strake thee with Stella's rays,
   Reason, thou kneel'dst, and offered'st straight to prove
   By reason good, good reason her to love.

7 (xv)

You that do search for every purling spring
  Which from the ribs of old Parnassus flows,
  And every flower, not sweet perhaps, which grows
  Near thereabout, into your poesy wring;
You that do dictionary's method bring
  Into your rhymes, running in rattling rows;
  You that poor Petrarch's long-deceasèd woes
  With new-born sighs and denizened wit do sing:
You take wrong ways; those far-fet helps be such
  As do bewray a want of inward touch;
  And sure, at length stolen goods do come to light.
But if, both for your love and skill, your name
  You seek to nurse at fullest breasts of fame,
  Stella behold, and then begin to indite.

8 (xvii)

His mother dear Cupid offended late,
  Because that Mars, grown slacker in her love,
  With pricking shot he did not throughly move
  To keep the pace of their first loving state.
The boy refused for fear of Mars's hate,
  Who threatened stripes if he his wrath did prove;
  But she in chafe him from her lap did shove,
  Brake bow, brake shafts, while Cupid weeping sate.
Till that his granddame Nature, pitying it,
  Of Stella's brows made him two better bows,
  And in her eyes, of arrows infinite.
O, how for joy he leaps, O, how he crows!
  And straight therewith, like wags new got to play,
  Falls to shrewd turns; and I was in his way.

9 (XVIII)

With what sharp checks I in myself am shent
   When into Reason's audit I do go,
   And by just counts myself a bankrupt know
Of all those goods which Heaven to me have lent;
Unable quite to pay even Nature's rent,
   Which unto it by birthright I do owe,
   And which is worse, no good excuse can show
But that my wealth I have most idly spent.
My youth doth waste, my knowledge brings forth toys;
   My wit doth strive those passions to defend
   Which for reward spoil it with vain annoys.
I see my course to lose myself doth bend;
   I see, and yet no greater sorrow take
   Than that I lose no more for Stella's sake.

10 (XX)

Fly, fly, my friends, I have my death-wound; fly;
   See there that boy, that murdering boy, I say,
   Who, like a thief, hid in dark bush doth lie
Till bloody bullet get him wrongful prey.
So, tyrant, he no fitter place could spy,
   Nor so fair level in so secret stay,
   As that sweet black which veils the heavenly eye;
There himself with his shot he close doth lay.
Poor passenger, pass now thereby I did,
   And stayed, pleased with the prospect of the place,
   While that black hue from me the bad guest hid:
But straight I saw motions of lightning grace,
   And then descried the glistering of his dart:
   But ere I could fly thence, it pierced my heart.

11 (XXI)

Your words, my friend, right healthful caustics, blame
  My young mind marred, whom Love doth windlass so
  That mine own writings, like bad servants, show
  My wits quick in vain thoughts, in virtue lame;
That Plato I read for nought but if he tame
  Such coltish gyres; that to my birth I owe
  Nobler desires, lest else that friendly foe,
  Great expectation, wear a train of shame.
For since mad March great promise made of me,
  If now the May of my years much decline,
  What can be hoped my harvest time will be?
Sure, you say well, your wisdom's golden mine
  Dig deep with learning's spade: now tell me this,
  Hath this world aught so fair as Stella is?

12 (XXIV)

Rich fools there be whose base and filthy heart
  Lies hatching still the goods wherein they flow,
  And, damning their own selves to Tantal's smart,
  Wealth breeding want, more blissed, more wretched grow.
Yet to those fools heaven such wit doth impart
  As, what their hands do hold, their heads do know,
  And knowing, love, and loving, lay apart
  As sacred things, far from all danger's show.
But that rich fool who by blind fortune's lot
  The richest gem of love and life enjoys,
  And can with foul abuse such beauties blot,
Let him, deprived of sweet but unfelt joys,
  Exiled for aye from those high treasures which
  He knows not, grow in only folly rich.

13 (XXVIII)

You that with allegory's curious frame
    Of others' children changelings use to make,
    With me those pains, for God's sake, do not take:
    I list not dig so deep for brazen fame.
When I say Stella, I do mean the same
    Princess of beauty, for whose only sake
    The reins of Love I love, though never slake,
    And joy therein, though nations count it shame.
I beg no subject to use eloquence,
    Nor in hid ways to guide philosophy;
    Look at my hands for no such quintessence;
But know that I in pure simplicity
    Breathe out the flames which burn within my heart,
    Love only reading unto me this art.

14 (XXX)

Whether the Turkish new moon minded be
    To fill his horns this year on Christian coast;
    How Poles' right king means, without leave of host,
    To warm with ill-made fire cold Muscovy;
If French can yet three parts in one agree;
    What now the Dutch in their full diets boast;
    How Holland hearts, now so good towns be lost,
    Trust in the shade of pleasing Orange tree;
How Ulster likes of that same golden bit
    Wherewith my father once made it half tame;
    If in the Scottish court be weltering yet:
These questions busy wits to me do frame;
    I, cumbered with good manners, answer do,
    But know not how, for still I think of you.

15 (XXXI)

With how sad steps, O Moon, thou climb'st the skies;
　　How silently, and with how wan a face;
　　What, may it be that even in heavenly place
　　That busy archer his sharp arrows tries?
Sure, if that long-with-Love-acquainted eyes
　　Can judge of love, thou feel'st a lover's case;
　　I read it in thy looks; thy languished grace
　　To me that feel the like thy state descries.
Then even of fellowship, O Moon, tell me,
　　Is constant love deemed there but want of wit?
　　Are beauties there as proud as here they be?
Do they above love to be loved, and yet
　　Those lovers scorn whom that Love doth possess?
　　Do they call virtue there ungratefulness?

16 (XXXIII)

I might—unhappy word—O me, I might,
　　And then would not, or could not, see my bliss,
　　Till now, wrapped in a most infernal night,
　　I find how heavenly day, wretch, I did miss.
Heart, rent thyself, thou dost thyself but right;
　　No lovely Paris made thy Helen his;
　　No force, no fraud robbed thee of thy delight,
　　Nor Fortune of thy fortune author is.
But to myself myself did give the blow,
　　While too much wit, forsooth, so troubled me
　　That I respects for both our sakes must show;
And yet could not by rising morn foresee
　　How fair a day was near: O punished eyes,
　　That I had been more foolish, or more wise!

17 (XXXIV)

Come, let me write. 'And to what end?' To ease
    A burdened heart. 'How can words ease, which are
    The glasses of thy daily vexing care?'
    Oft cruel fights well pictured forth do please.
'Art not ashamed to publish thy disease?'
    Nay, that may breed my fame, it is so rare.
    'But will not wise men think thy words fond ware?'
    Then be they close, and so none shall displease.
'What idler thing than speak and not be heard?'
    What harder thing than smart and not to speak?
    Peace, foolish wit; with wit my wit is marred.
Thus write I, while I doubt to write, and wreak
    My harms in ink's poor loss. Perhaps some find
    Stella's great powers, that so confuse my mind.

18 (XXXIX)

Come Sleep, O Sleep, the certain knot of peace,
    The bating place of wit, the balm of woe,
    The poor man's wealth, the prisoner's release,
    The indifferent judge between the high and low;
With shield of proof shield me from out the prease
    Of those fierce darts Despair at me doth throw:
    O make in me those civil wars to cease:
    I will good tribute pay if thou do so.
Take thou of me smooth pillows, sweetest bed,
    A chamber deaf to noise and blind to light,
    A rosy garland and a weary head;
And if these things, as being thine by right,
    Move not thy heavy grace, thou shalt in me,
    Livelier than elsewhere, Stella's image see.

19 (XL)

As good to write as for to lie and groan.
  O Stella dear, how much thy power hath wrought,
  That hast my mind, none of the basest, brought,
  My still-kept course, while others sleep, to moan.
Alas, if from the height of virtue's throne
  Thou canst vouchsafe the influence of a thought
  Upon a wretch that long thy grace hath sought,
  Weigh then how I by thee am overthrown.
And then think thus: although thy beauty be
  Made manifest by such a victory,
  Yet noblest conquerors do wrecks avoid.
Since then thou hast so far subduèd me
  That in my heart I offer still to thee,
  O, do not let thy temple be destroyed.

20 (XLVII)

What, have I thus betrayed my liberty?
  Can those black beams such burning marks engrave
  In my free side, or am I born a slave
  Whose neck becomes such yoke of tyranny?
Or want I sense to feel my misery,
  Or sprite, disdain of such disdain to have,
  Who for long faith, though daily help I crave,
  May get no alms but scorn of beggary?
Virtue, awake; beauty but beauty is.
  I may, I must, I can, I will, I do
  Leave following that which it is gain to miss.
Let her go.—Soft, but here she comes. Go to,
  Unkind, I love you not! O me, that eye
  Doth make my heart give to my tongue the lie.

21 (XLVIII)

Soul's joy, bend not those morning stars from me
   Where virtue is made strong by beauty's might:
   Where love is chasteness, pain doth learn delight,
   And humbleness grows one with majesty.
Whatever may ensue, O let me be
   Co-partner of the riches of that sight;
   Let not mine eyes be hell-driven from that light;
   O look, O shine, O let me die, and see.
For though I oft myself of them bemoan
   That through my heart their beamy darts be gone
   Whose cureless wounds even now most freshly bleed,
Yet since my death-wound is already got,
   Dear killer, spare not thy sweet-cruel shot:
   A kind of grace it is to slay with speed.

22 (LIII)

In martial sports I had my cunning tried,
   And yet to break more staves did me address,
   While with the people's shouts, I must confess,
   Youth, luck, and praise even filled my veins with pride,
When Cupid, having me, his slave, descried
   In Mars's livery prancing in the press,
   'What now, sir fool,' said he, 'I would no less!
   Look here, I say!' I looked, and Stella spied,
Who hard by made a window send forth light.
   My heart then quaked, then dazzled were mine eyes,
   One hand forgot to rule, the other to fight.
Nor trumpet's sound I heard, nor friendly cries:
   My foe came on, and beat the air for me,
   Till that her blush taught me my shame to see.

23 (LXII)

Late tired with woe, even ready for to pine
  With rage of love, I called my love unkind;
  She in whose eyes Love, though unfelt, doth shine
  Sweet, said that I true love in her should find.
I joyed; but straight thus watered was my wine:
  That love she did, but loved a love not blind,
  Which would not let me, whom she loved, decline
  From nobler course fit for my birth and mind;
And therefore by her love's authority
  Willed me these tempests of vain love to fly,
  And anchor fast myself on Virtue's shore.
Alas, if this the only metal be
  Of Love, new-coined to help my beggary,
  Dear, love me not, that you may love me more.

24 (LXIV)

No more, my dear, no more these counsels try;
  O, give my passions leave to run their race;
  Let fortune lay on me her worst disgrace;
  Let folk o'ercharged with brain against me cry;
Let clouds bedim my face, break in mine eye;
  Let me no steps but of lost labour trace;
  Let all the earth with scorn recount my case;
  But do not will me from my love to fly.
I do not envy Aristotle's wit,
  Nor do aspire to Caesar's bleeding fame,
  Nor aught do care though some above me sit,
Nor hope nor wish another course to frame,
  But that which once may win thy cruel heart:
  Thou art my wit, and thou my virtue art.

25 (LXVI)

And do I see some cause a hope to feed,
   Or doth the tedious burden of long woe
   In weakened minds quick apprehending breed
   Of every image which may comfort show?
I cannot brag of word, much less of deed;
   Fortune's wheel's still with me in one sort slow;
   My wealth no more, and no whit less my need;
   Desire still on the stilts of fear doth go.
And yet amid all fears a hope there is,
   Stolen to my heart since last fair night, nay, day;
   Stella's eyes sent to me the beams of bliss,
Looking on me while I looked other way:
   But when mine eyes back to their heaven did move,
   They fled with blush which guilty seemed of love.

26 (LXVIII)

Stella, the only planet of my light,
   Light of my life, and life of my desire,
   Chief good whereto my hope doth only aspire,
   World of my wealth and heaven of my delight,
Why dost thou spend the treasures of thy sprite
   With voice more fit to wed Amphion's lyre,
   Seeking to quench in me the noble fire
   Fed by thy worth, and blinded by thy sight?
And all in vain: for while thy breath most sweet
   With choicest words, thy words with reasons rare,
   Thy reasons firmly set on virtue's feet,
Labour to kill in me this killing care,
   O, think I then what paradise of joy
   It is, so fair a virtue to enjoy.

27 (LXIX)

O joy, too high for my low style to show!
  O bliss, fit for a nobler state than me!
  Envy, put out thine eyes, lest thou do see
  What oceans of delight in me do flow!
My friend, that oft saw through all masks my woe,
  Come, come, and let me pour myself on thee;
  Gone is the winter of my misery,
  My spring appears; O, see what here doth grow!
For Stella hath, with words where faith doth shine,
  Of her high heart given me the monarchy:
  I, I, oh I may say that she is mine.
And though she give but thus condition'ly
  This realm of bliss while virtuous course I take,
  No kings be crowned but they some covenants make.

28 (LXXI)

Who will in fairest book of nature know
  How virtue may best lodged in beauty be,
  Let him but learn of love to read in thee,
  Stella, those fair lines which true goodness show.
There shall he find all vices' overthrow,
  Not by rude force, but sweetest sovereignty
  Of reason, from whose light those night-birds fly,
  That inward sun in thine eyes shineth so.
And, not content to be perfection's heir
  Thyself, dost strive all minds that way to move
  Who mark in thee what is in thee most fair.
So, while thy beauty draws the heart to love,
  As fast thy virtue bends that love to good:
  But ah, desire still cries, 'Give me some food'.

29 (LXXIV)

I never drank of Aganippe well,
  Nor ever did in shade of Tempe sit,
  And Muses scorn with vulgar brains to dwell;
  Poor layman I, for sacred rites unfit.
Some do I hear of poets' fury tell,
  But, God wot, wot not what they mean by it;
  And this I swear by blackest brook of hell,
  I am no pick-purse of another's wit.
How falls it, then, that with so smooth an ease
  My thoughts I speak, and what I speak doth flow
  In verse, and that my verse best wits doth please?
Guess we the cause. 'What, is it thus?' Fie, no.
  'Or so?' Much less. 'How then?' Sure, thus it is:
  My lips are sweet, inspired with Stella's kiss.

30 (LXXVI)

She comes, and straight therewith her shining twins do move
  Their rays to me, who in her tedious absence lay
  Benighted in cold woe; but now appears my day,
  The only light of joy, the only warmth of love.
She comes with light and warmth which, like Aurora, prove
  Of gentle force, so that mine eyes dare gladly play
  With such a rosy morn, whose beams most freshly gay
  Scorch not, but only do dark chilling sprites remove.
But lo, while I do speak, it groweth noon with me;
  Her flamy glistering lights increase with time and place;
  My heart cries 'ah', it burns, mine eyes now dazzled be;
No wind, no shade can cool: what help then in my case?
  But with short breath, long looks, stayed feet, and walking
    head,
  Pray that my sun go down with meeker beams to bed.

31 (LXXVIII)

O, how the pleasant airs of true love be
  Infected by those vapours which arise
  From out that noisome gulf which gaping lies
  Between the jaws of hellish jealousy!
A monster, others' harm, self-misery,
  Beauty's plague, virtue's scourge, succour of lies,
  Who his own joy to his own hurt applies,
  And only cherish doth with injury.
Who, since he hath by nature's special grace,
  So piercing paws as spoil when they embrace,
  So nimble feet as stir still, though on thorns,
So many eyes aye seeking their own woe,
  So ample ears as never good news know:
  Is it not evil that such a devil wants horns?

32 (LXXXI)

O kiss, which dost those ruddy gems impart,
  Or gems, or fruits of new-found paradise,
  Breathing all bliss and sweetening to the heart,
  Teaching dumb lips a nobler exercise;
O kiss, which souls, even souls, together ties
  By links of love and only nature's art,
  How fain would I paint thee to all men's eyes,
  Or of thy gifts at least shade out some part.
But she forbids: with blushing words she says
  She builds her fame on higher-seated praise.
  But my heart burns; I cannot silent be.
Then since, dear life, you fain would have me peace,
  And I, mad with delight, want wit to cease,
  Stop you my mouth with still still kissing me.

33 (LXXXIII)

Good brother Philip, I have borne you long;
  I was content you should in favour creep,
  While craftily you seemed your cut to keep,
  As though that fair soft hand did you great wrong.
I bare, with envy, yet I bare your song,
  When in her neck you did love-ditties peep;
  Nay, more fool I, oft suffered you to sleep
  In lilies' nest where Love's self lies along.
What, doth high place ambitious thoughts augment?
  Is sauciness reward of courtesy?
  Cannot such grace your silly self content
But you must needs with those lips billing be,
  And through those lips drink nectar from that tongue?
  Leave that, Sir Phip, lest off your neck be wrung!

34 (LXXXIV)

Highway, since you my chief Parnassus be,
  And that my Muse, to some ears not unsweet,
  Tempers her words to trampling horses' feet
  More oft than to a chamber-melody,
Now blessèd you bear onward blessèd me
  To her where I my heart safeliest shall meet:
  My Muse and I must you of duty greet
  With thanks and wishes, wishing thankfully.
Be you still fair, honoured by public heed,
  By no encroachment wronged nor time forgot,
  Nor blamed for blood, nor shamed for sinful deed;
And, that you know I envy you no lot
  Of highest wish, I wish you so much bliss,
  Hundreds of years you Stella's feet may kiss.

35 (LXXXV)

I see the house: my heart, thyself contain:
 Beware full sails drown not thy tottering barge,
 Lest joy, by nature apt sprites to enlarge,
 Thee to thy wreck beyond thy limits strain.
Nor do like lords whose weak confusèd brain,
 Not pointing to fit folks each under charge,
 While every office themselves will discharge,
 With doing all, leave nothing done but pain.
But give apt servants their due place: let eyes
 See beauty's total sum summed in her face;
 Let ears hear speech which wit to wonder ties;
Let breath suck up those sweets; let arms embrace
 The globe of weal, lips love's indentures make:
 Thou but of all the kingly tribute take.

36 (LXXXVII)

When I was forced from Stella ever dear,
 Stella, food of my thoughts, heart of my heart,
 Stella, whose eyes make all my tempests clear,
 By iron laws of duty to depart:
Alas, I found that she with me did smart;
 I saw that tears did in her eyes appear;
 I saw that sighs her sweetest lips did part,
 And her sad words my saddest sense did hear.
For me, I wept to see pearls scattered so,
 I sighed her sighs, and wailèd for her woe,
 Yet swam in joy, such love in her was seen.
Thus, while the effect most bitter was to me,
 And nothing than the cause more sweet could be,
 I had been vexed if vexed I had not been.

37 (XCI)

Stella, while now by honour's cruel might
  I am from you, light of my life, misled,
  And that fair you, my sun, thus overspread
  With absence' veil, I live in sorrow's night,
If this dark place yet show like candle-light
  Some beauty's piece, as amber-coloured head,
  Milk hands, rose cheeks, or lips more sweet, more red,
  Or seeing jets black, but in blackness bright,
They please, I do confess, they please mine eyes;
  But why? Because of you they models be;
  Models such be wood-globes of glistering skies.
Dear, therefore be not jealous over me
  If you hear that they seem my heart to move.
  Not them, O no, but you in them I love.

38 (XCII)

Be your words made, good sir, of Indian ware,
  That you allow me them by so small rate?
  Or do you cutted Spartans imitate?
  Or do you mean my tender ears to spare,
That to my questions you so total are?
  When I demand of Phoenix Stella's state
  You say, forsooth, you left her well of late:
  O God, think you that satisfies my care?
I would know whether she did sit or walk;
  How clothed; how waited on; sighed she, or smiled;
  Whereof, with whom, how often did she talk;
With what pastime time's journey she beguiled;
  If her lips deigned to sweeten my poor name.
  Say all, and, all well said, still say the same.

39 (CI)

Stella is sick, and in that sick-bed lies
    Sweetness which breathes and pants as oft as she;
    And Grace, sick too, such fine conclusion tries
    That Sickness brags itself best graced to be.
Beauty is sick, but sick in so fair guise
    That in that paleness Beauty's white we see,
    And Joy, which is inseparate from those eyes,
    Stella now learns, strange case, to weep in thee.
Love moans thy pain, and like a faithful page,
    As thy looks stir, runs up and down to make
    All folks prest at thy will thy pain to assuage;
Nature with care sweats for her darling's sake,
    Knowing worlds pass ere she enough can find
    Of such heaven stuff to clothe so heavenly a mind.

40 (CIII)

O happy Thames that didst my Stella bear,
    I saw thyself with many a smiling line
    Upon thy cheerful face joy's livery wear,
    While those fair planets on thy streams did shine.
The boat for joy could not to dance forbear,
    While wanton winds, with beauties so divine
    Ravished, stayed not till in her golden hair
    They did themselves, O sweetest prison, twine.
And fain those Aeol's youths there would their stay
    Have made, but forced by Nature still to fly,
    First did with puffing kiss those locks display.
She, so dishevelled, blushed; from window I
    With sight thereof cried out: 'O fair disgrace,
    Let honour' self to thee grant highest place'.

41 (CV)

Unhappy sight, and hath she vanished by
   So near, in so good time, so free a place?
   Dead glass, dost thou thy object so embrace
   As what my heart still sees thou canst not spy?
I swear, by her I live and lack, that I
   Was not in fault, who bent thy dazzling race
   Only unto the heaven of Stella's face,
   Counting but dust what in the way did lie.
But cease: mine eyes, your tears do witness well
   That you, guiltless thereof, your nectar missed.
   Cursed be the page from whom the bad torch fell:
Cursed be the night which did your strife resist:
   Cursed be the coachman that did drive so fast,
   With no worse curse than absence makes me taste.

42 (CVII)

Stella, since thou so right a princess art
   Of all the powers which life bestows on me,
   That, ere by them aught undertaken be,
   They first resort unto that sovereign part;
Sweet, for a while give respite to my heart,
   Which pants as though it still should leap to thee,
   And on my thoughts give thy lieutenancy
   To this great cause, which needs both use and art.
And as a queen, who from her presence sends
   Whom she employs, dismiss from thee my wit,
   Till it have wrought what thy own will attends.
On servants' shame oft master's blame doth sit:
   O, let not fools in me thy works reprove,
   And scorning say, 'See what it is to love!'

[OTHER SONNETS]
43

Thou blind man's mark, thou fool's self-chosen snare,
    Fond fancy's scum, and dregs of scattered thought,
    Band of all evils, cradle of causeless care,
    Thou web of will, whose end is never wrought:
Desire, desire, I have too dearly bought
    With price of mangled mind thy worthless ware;
    Too long, too long asleep thou hast me brought,
    Who should my mind to higher things prepare.
But yet in vain thou hast my ruin sought;
    In vain thou mad'st me to vain things aspire;
    In vain thou kindlest all thy smoky fire:
For virtue hath this better lesson taught,
    Within myself to seek my only hire;
    Desiring naught but how to kill desire.

44

Leave me, O love which reachest but to dust,
    And thou, my mind, aspire to higher things;
    Grow rich in that which never taketh rust;
    Whatever fades, but fading pleasure brings.
Draw in thy beams, and humble all thy might
    To that sweet yoke where lasting freedoms be;
    Which breaks the clouds and opens forth the light,
    That doth both shine and give us sight to see.
O, take fast hold, let that light be thy guide
    In this small course which birth draws out to death;
    And think how evil becometh him to slide
Who seeketh heaven, and comes of heavenly breath.
    Then farewell world; thy uttermost I see;
    Eternal love, maintain thy life in me.

Splendidis longum valedico nugis.

EDMUND SPENSER (1552?–99)

Amoretti

1 (I)

Happy ye leaves, whenas those lily hands,
    which hold my life in their dead-doing might,
    shall handle you, and hold in love's soft bands
    like captives trembling at the victors' sight;
And happy lines, on which with starry light
    those lamping eyes will deign sometimes to look,
    and read the sorrows of my dying sprite,
    written with tears in heart's close-bleeding book;
And happy rhymes, bathed in the sacred brook
    of Helicon, whence she derivèd is,
    when ye behold that angel's blessed look,
    my soul's long-lackèd food, my heaven's bliss.
Leaves, lines, and rhymes, seek her to please alone,
    whom if ye please, I care for other none.

2 (II)

Unquiet thought, whom at the first I bred
    of th'inward bale of my love-pinèd heart,
    and sithence have with sighs and sorrows fed
    till greater than my womb thou waxen art:
Break forth at length out of the inner part
    in which thou lurkest, like to viper's brood,
    and seek some succour both to ease my smart
    and also to sustain thyself with food.
But if in presence of that fairest proud
    thou chance to come, fall lowly at her feet,
    and with meek humblesse and afflicted mood
    pardon for thee, and grace for me, entreat.
Which if she grant, then live, and my love cherish;
    if not, die soon, and I with thee will perish.

3 (III)

The sovereign beauty which I do admire,
  witness the world how worthy to be praised:
  the light whereof hath kindled heavenly fire
  in my frail spirit, by her from baseness raised:
That being now with her huge brightness dazed,
  base thing I can no more endure to view;
  but looking still on her, I stand amazed
  at wondrous sight of so celestial hue.
So, when my tongue would speak her praises due,
  it stoppèd is with thoughts' astonishment;
  and when my pen would write her titles true,
  it ravished is with fancy's wonderment.
Yet in my heart I then both speak and write
  the wonder that my wit cannot indite.

4 (IV)

New year, forth looking out of Janus' gate,
  doth seem to promise hope of new delight,
  and bidding th' old adieu, his passèd date
  bids all old thoughts to die in dumpish sprite;
  And calling forth out of sad winter's night
  fresh Love, that long hath slept in cheerless bower,
bids him awake and soon about him dight
  his wanton wings and darts of deadly power.
For lusty spring, now in his timely hour,
  is ready to come forth him to receive,
  and warns the earth with divers coloured flower
  to deck herself, and her fair mantle weave.
Then you, fair flower, in whom fresh youth doth reign,
  prepare yourself new love to entertain.

5 (v)

Rudely thou wrongest my dear heart's desire
  in finding fault with her too portly pride:
  the thing which I do most in her admire
  is of the world unworthy most envied.
For in those lofty looks is close implied
  scorn of base things, and 'sdain of foul dishonour,
  threat'ning rash eyes which gaze on her so wide,
  that loosely they ne dare to look upon her.
Such pride is praise, such portliness is honour,
  that boldened innocence bears in her eyes;
  and her fair countenance like a goodly banner
  spreads in defiance of all enemies.
Was never in this world aught worthy tried
  without some spark of such self-pleasing pride.

6 (viii)

More than most fair, full of the living fire,
  kindled above unto the Maker near;
  no eyes but joys, in which all powers conspire
  that to the world naught else be counted dear:
Through your bright beams doth not the blinded guest
  shoot out his darts to base affections' wound,
  but angels come to lead frail minds to rest
  in chaste desires, on heavenly beauty bound.
You frame my thoughts and fashion me within;
  you stop my tongue, and teach my heart to speak;
  you calm the storm that passion did begin;
  strong through your cause, but by your virtue weak.
Dark is the world where your light shinèd never;
  well is he born, that may behold you ever.

7 (XIII)

In that proud port, which her so goodly graceth,
    whiles her fair face she rears up to the sky,
    and to the ground her eyelids low embaseth,
    most goodly temperature ye may descry,
Mild humblesse mixed with awful majesty.
    For looking on the earth whence she was born,
    her mind remembreth her mortality,
    what so is fairest shall to earth return.
But that same lofty countenance seems to scorn
    base thing, and think how she to heaven may climb,
    treading down earth as loathsome and forlorn,
    that hinders heavenly thoughts with drossy slime.
Yet lowly still vouchsafe to look on me;
    such lowliness shall make you lofty be.

8 (xv)

Ye tradeful merchants that with weary toil
    do seek most precious things to make your gain,
    and both the Indias of their treasures spoil,
    what needeth you to seek so far in vain?
For lo, my love doth in herself contain
    all this world's riches that may fair be found;
    if sapphires, lo her eyes be sapphires plain;
    if rubies, lo her lips be rubies sound;
If pearls, her teeth be pearls both pure and round;
    if ivory, her forehead ivory ween;
    if gold, her locks are finest gold on ground;
    if silver, her fair hands are silver sheen.
But that which fairest is, but few behold,
    her mind adorned with virtues manifold.

9 (XIX)

The merry cuckoo, messenger of spring,
    his trumpet shrill hath thrice already sounded,
    that warns all lovers wait upon their king,
    who now is coming forth with garland crownèd;
With noise whereof the choir of birds resounded
    their anthems sweet devisèd of Love's praise,
    that all the woods their echoes back rebounded
    as if they knew the meaning of their lays.
But 'mongst them all which did Love's honour raise
    no word was heard of her that most it ought;
    but she his precept proudly disobeys,
    and doth his idle message set at naught.
Therefore, O Love, unless she turn to thee
    ere cuckoo end, let her a rebel be.

10 (XXII)

This holy season fit to fast and pray,
    men to devotion ought to be inclined:
    therefore I likewise on so holy day
    for my sweet saint some service fit will find.
Her temple fair is built within my mind,
    in which her glorious image placèd is,
    on which my thoughts do day and night attend
    like sacred priests that never think amiss.
There I to her as the author of my bliss
    will build an altar to appease her ire;
    and on the same my heart will sacrifice,
    burning in flames of pure and chaste desire:
The which vouchsafe, O goddess, to accept,
    amongst thy dearest relics to be kept.

11 (XXIII)

Penelope for her Ulysses' sake
    devised a web her wooers to deceive,
    in which the work that she all day did make
    the same at night she did again unreave.
Such subtle craft my damsel doth conceive
    the importune suit of my desire to shun:
    for all that I in many days do weave,
    in one short hour I find by her undone.
So, when I think to end that I begun,
    I must begin, and never bring to end;
    for with one look she spills that long I spun,
    and with one word my whole year's work doth rend.
Such labour like the spider's web I find,
    whose fruitless work is broken with least wind.

12 (XXVII)

Fair proud, now tell me why should fair be proud,
    sith all world's glory is but dross unclean,
    and in the shade of death itself shall shroud,
    however now thereof ye little ween.
That goodly idol now so gay beseen
    shall doff her flesh's borrowed fair attire,
    and be forgot as it had never been,
    that many now much worship and admire.
Ne any then shall after it inquire,
    ne any mention shall thereof remain,
    but what this verse, that never shall expire,
    shall to you purchase with her thankless pain.
Fair, be no longer proud of that shall perish,
    but that which shall you make immortal, cherish.

13 (XXXIII)

Great wrong I do, I can it not deny,
    to that most sacred Empress, my dear dread,
    not finishing her Queen of Faery,
    that mote enlarge her living praises, dead;
But, Lodwick, this of grace to me aread:
    do ye not think the accomplishment of it
    sufficient work for one man's simple head,
    all were it, as the rest, but rudely writ?
How then should I without another wit
    think ever to endure so tedious toil,
    since that this one is tossed with troublous fit
    of a proud love, that doth my spirit spoil?
Cease then, till she vouchsafe to grant me rest,
    or lend you me another living breast.

14 (XXXIV)

Like as a ship that through the ocean wide
    by conduct of some star doth make her way,
    whenas a storm hath dimmed her trusty guide,
    out of her course doth wander far astray,
So I, whose star that wont with her bright ray
    me to direct, with clouds is overcast,
    do wander now in darkness and dismay
    through hidden perils round about me placed.
Yet hope I well that when this storm is past
    my Helicè, the lodestar of my life,
    will shine again and look on me at last
    with lovely light to clear my cloudy grief.
Till then I wander careful comfortless,
    in secret sorrow and sad pensiveness.

15 (XL)

Mark when she smiles with amiable cheer,
  and tell me whereto can ye liken it,
  when on each eyelid sweetly do appear
  an hundred graces as in shade to sit.
Likest it seemeth in my simple wit
  unto the fair sunshine in summer's day,
  that, when a dreadful storm away is flit,
  through the broad world doth spread his goodly ray:
At sight whereof each bird that sits on spray,
  and every beast that to his den was fled,
  comes forth afresh out of their late dismay
  and to the light lift up their drooping head.
So my storm-beaten heart likewise is cheered
  with that sunshine when cloudy looks are cleared.

16 (LI)

Do I not see that fairest images
  of hardest marble are of purpose made,
  for that they should endure through many ages,
  ne let their famous monuments to fade?
Why then do I, untrained in lovers' trade,
  her hardness blame which I should more commend,
  sith never aught was excellent assayed
  which was not hard t'achieve and bring to end?
Ne aught so hard, but he that would attend
  mote soften it and to his will allure;
  so do I hope her stubborn heart to bend,
  and that it then more steadfast will endure.
Only my pains will be the more to get her;
  but having her, my joy will be the greater.

17 (LVIII)

Weak is th'assurance that weak flesh reposeth
  in her own power, and scorneth others' aid:
  that soonest falls whenas she most supposeth
  herself assured, and is of nought afraid.
All flesh is frail, and all her strength unstaid,
  like a vain bubble blowen up with air:
  devouring time and changeful chance have preyed
  her glory's pride, that none may it repair.
Ne none so rich or wise, so strong or fair,
  but faileth, trusting on his own assurance:
  and he that standeth on the highest stair
  falls lowest; for on earth nought hath endurance.
Why then do ye, proud fair, misdeem so far,
  that to yourself ye most assurèd are?

18 (LIX)

Thrice happy she, that is so well assured
  unto herself, and settled so in heart;
  that neither will for better be allured,
  ne feared with worse to any chance to start;
But like a steady ship doth strongly part
  the raging waves, and keeps her course aright,
  ne aught for tempest doth from it depart,
  ne aught for fairer weather's false delight.
Such self-assurance need not fear the spite
  of grudging foes, ne favour seek of friends,
  but in the stay of her own steadfast might
  neither to one herself nor other bends.
Most happy she that most assured doth rest,
  but he most happy who such one loves best.

19 (LX)

They that in course of heavenly spheres are skilled
  to every planet point his sundry year,
  in which her circle's voyage is fulfilled,
  as Mars in three-score years doth run his sphere.
So, since the wingèd god his planet clear
  began in me to move, one year is spent;
  the which doth longer unto me appear
  than all those forty which my life outwent.
Then, by that count which lovers' books invent,
  the sphere of Cupid forty years contains;
  which I have wasted in long languishment
  that seemed the longer for my greater pains.
But let my love's fair planet short her ways
  this year ensuing, or else short my days.

20 (LXI)

The glorious image of the Maker's beauty,
  my sovereign saint, the idol of my thought,
  dare not henceforth above the bounds of duty
  to accuse of pride, or rashly blame for aught.
For being as she is divinely wrought,
  and of the brood of angels heavenly born,
  and with the crew of blessèd saints upbrought,
  each of which did her with their gifts adorn,
The bud of joy, the blossom of the morn,
  the beam of light whom mortal eyes admire,
  what reason is it then but she should scorn
  base things that to her love too bold aspire?
Such heavenly forms ought rather worshipped be
  than dare be loved by men of mean degree.

21 (LXII)

The weary year his race now having run,
  the new begins his compassed course anew;
  with show of morning mild he hath begun,
  betokening peace and plenty to ensue.
So let us, which this change of weather view,
  change eke our minds and former lives amend;
  the old year's sins forepast let us eschew,
  and fly the faults with which we did offend.
Then shall the new year's joy forth freshly send
  into the glooming world his gladsome ray,
  and all these storms which now his beauty blend
  shall turn to calms, and timely clear away.
So likewise, love, cheer you your heavy sprite,
  and change old year's annoy to new delight.

22 (LXIII)

After long storms and tempests' sad assay,
  which hardly I endurèd heretofore,
  in dread of death and dangerous dismay,
  with which my silly bark was tossèd sore,
I do at length descry the happy shore
  in which I hope ere long for to arrive;
  fair soil it seems from far, and fraught with store
  of all that dear and dainty is alive.
Most happy he that can at last achieve
  the joyous safety of so sweet a rest,
  whose least delight sufficeth to deprive
  remembrance of all pains which him oppressed.
All pains are nothing in respect of this;
  all sorrows short that gain eternal bliss.

23 (LXIV)

Coming to kiss her lips—such grace I found—
  meseemed I smelt a garden of sweet flowers,
  that dainty odours from them threw around
  for damsels fit to deck their lovers' bowers.
Her lips did smell like unto gillyflowers,
  her ruddy cheeks like unto roses red,
  her snowy brows like budded belamours,
  her lovely eyes like pinks but newly spread;
her goodly bosom like a strawberry bed,
  her neck like to a bunch of columbines,
  her breast like lilies ere their leaves be shed,
  her nipples like young blossomed jessamines.
Such fragrant flowers do give most odorous smell,
  but her sweet odour did them all excel.

24 (LXVII)

Like as a huntsman after weary chase,
  seeing the game from him escaped away,
  sits down to rest him in some shady place
  with panting hounds beguilèd of their prey,
So after long pursuit and vain assay,
  when I all weary had the chase forsook,
  the gentle deer returned the selfsame way,
  thinking to quench her thirst at the next brook.
There she, beholding me with milder look,
  sought not to fly, but fearless still did bide;
  till I in hand her, yet half trembling, took,
  and with her own goodwill her firmly tied.
Strange thing meseemed to see a beast so wild
  so goodly won, with her own will beguiled.

25 (LXVIII)

Most glorious Lord of life, that on this day
    didst make thy triumph over death and sin,
    and having harrowed hell, didst bring away
    captivity, thence captive us to win:
This joyous day, dear Lord, with joy begin,
    and grant that we for whom thou didest die,
    being with thy dear blood clean washed from sin,
    may live for ever in felicity:
And that thy love we weighing worthily,
    may likewise love thee for the same again,
    and for thy sake, that all like dear didst buy,
    with love may one another entertain.
So let us love, dear love, like as we ought;
    love is the lesson which the Lord us taught.

26 (LXX)

Fresh spring, the herald of Love's mighty king,
    in whose coat-armour richly are displayed
    all sorts of flowers the which on earth do spring,
    in goodly colours gloriously arrayed:
Go to my love where she is careless laid,
    yet in her winter's bower not well awake:
    tell her the joyous time will not be stayed,
    unless she do him by the forelock take.
Bid her therefore herself soon ready make
    to wait on Love amongst his lovely crew,
    where everyone that misseth then her make
    shall be by him amerced with penance due.
Make haste, therefore, sweet love, whilst it is prime,
    for none can call again the passèd time.

27 (LXXII)

Oft when my spirit doth spread her bolder wings
  in mind to mount up to the purest sky,
    it down is weighed with thought of earthly things
    and clogged with burden of mortality;
Where, when that sovereign beauty it doth spy,
  resembling heaven's glory in her light,
    drawn with sweet pleasure's bait it back doth fly,
    and unto heaven forgets her former flight.
There my frail fancy fed with full delight
  doth bathe in bliss, and mantleth most at ease;
    ne thinks of other heaven but how it might
    her heart's desire with most contentment please.
Heart need not with none other happiness
  but here on earth to have such heaven's bliss.

28 (LXXIV)

Most happy letters framed by skilful trade,
  with which that happy name was first designed,
    the which three times thrice happy hath me made
    with gifts of body, fortune, and of mind!
The first my being to me gave by kind,
  from mother's womb derived by due descent;
    the second is my sovereign queen most kind,
    that honour and large richesse to me lent;
The third my love, my life's last ornament,
  by whom my spirit out of dust was raised,
    to speak her praise and glory excellent,
    of all alive most worthy to be praised.
Ye three Elizabeths, for ever live,
  that three such graces did unto me give.

29 (LXXVI)

Fair bosom fraught with virtue's richest treasure,
    the nest of love, the lodging of delight,
    the bower of bliss, the paradise of pleasure,
    the sacred harbour of that heavenly sprite:
How was I ravished with your lovely sight,
    and my frail thoughts too rashly led astray;
    whiles, diving deep through amorous insight,
    on the sweet spoil of beauty they did prey!
And twixt her paps like early fruit in May,
    whose harvest seemed to hasten now apace,
    they loosely did their wanton wings display,
    and there to rest themselves did boldly place.
Sweet thoughts, I envy your so happy rest,
    which oft I wished, yet never was so blessed.

30 (LXXVII)

Was it a dream, or did I see it plain,
    a goodly table of pure ivory
    all spread with junkets, fit to entertain
    the greatest prince with pompous royalty?
'Mongst which there in a silver dish did lie
    two golden apples of unvalued price,
    far passing those which Hercules came by,
    or those which Atalanta did entice:
Exceeding sweet, yet void of sinful vice,
    that many sought, yet none could ever taste;
    sweet fruit of pleasure brought from paradise
    by Love himself, and in his garden placed.
Her breast that table was, so richly spread,
    my thoughts the guests, which would thereon have fed.

31 (LXXX)

After so long a race as I have run
   through faery land, which those six books compile,
   give leave to rest me, being half foredone,
   and gather to myself new breath a while;
Then, as a steed refreshèd after toil,
   out of my prison I will break anew,
   and stoutly will that second work assoil
   with strong endeavour and attention due.
Till then, give leave to me in pleasant mew
   to sport my muse, and sing my love's sweet praise,
   the contemplation of whose heavenly hue
   my spirit to a higher pitch will raise.
But let her praises yet be low and mean,
   fit for the handmaid of the Faery Queen.

32 (LXXXIV)

Let not one spark of filthy lustful fire
   break out that may her sacred peace molest;
   ne one light glance of sensual desire
   attempt to work her gentle mind's unrest;
But pure affections bred in spotless breast,
   and modest thoughts breathed from well-tempered sprites,
   go visit her in her chaste bower of rest,
   accompanied with angelic delights.
There fill yourself with those most joyous sights
   the which myself could never yet attain;
   but speak no word to her of these sad plights
   which her too constant stiffness doth constrain.
Only behold her rare perfection,
   and bless your fortune's fair election.

33 (LXXXVI)

Venomous tongue, tipped with vile adder's sting,
   of that self kind with which the Furies fell
   their snaky heads do comb, from which a spring
   of poisoned words and spiteful speeches well:
Let all the plagues and horrid pains of hell
   upon thee fall for thine accursed hire,
   that with false forgèd lies which thou didst tell
   in my true love did stir up coals of ire:
The sparks whereof let kindle thine own fire,
   and catching hold of thine own wicked head
   consume thee quite, that didst with guile conspire
   in my sweet love such breaches to have bred.
Shame be thy meed and mischief thy reward,
   due to thyself, that it for me prepared!

34 (LXXXVIII)

Since I have lacked the comfort of that light
   the which was wont to lead my thoughts astray,
   I wander as in darkness of the night,
   afraid of every danger's least dismay.
Ne aught I see, though in the clearest day,
   when others gaze upon their shadows vain,
   but th'only image of that heavenly ray
   whereof some glance doth in mine eye remain:
Of which beholding the idea plain,
   through contemplation of my purest part,
   with light thereof I do myself sustain,
   and thereon feed my love-affamished heart.
But with such brightness whilst I fill my mind,
   I starve my body and mine eyes do blind.

SAMUEL DANIEL (1562–1619)

Delia

1

Look, Delia, how we steem the half-blown rose,
The image of thy blush and summer's honour,
Whilst in her tender green she doth enclose
That pure sweet beauty Time bestows upon her.
  No sooner spreads her glory in the air
But straight her full-blown pride is in declining;
She then is scorned that late adorned the fair:
So clouds thy beauty, after fairest shining.
  No April can revive thy withered flowers
Whose blooming grace adorns thy glory now:
Swift, speedy Time, feathered with flying hours,
Dissolves the beauty of the fairest brow.
    O let not then such riches waste in vain,
    But love whilst that thou mayst be loved again.

2

But love whilst that thou mayst be loved again,
Now, whilst thy May hath filled thy lap with flowers;
Now, whilst thy beauty bears without a stain;
Now use thy summer smiles ere winter lowers.
  And whilst thou spreadst unto the rising sun,
The fairest flower that ever saw the light,
Now joy thy time before thy sweet be done;
And, Delia, think thy morning must have night,
  And that thy brightness sets at length to west,
When thou wilt close up that which now thou showest;
And think the same becomes thy fading best
Which then shall hide it most, and cover lowest.
    Men do not weigh the stalk for that it was
    When once they find her flower, her glory pass.

3

When men shall find thy flower, thy glory pass,
And thou with careful brow, sitting alone,
Receivèd hast this message from thy glass,
That tells the truth, and says that all is gone:
    Fresh shalt thou see in me the wounds thou madest;
Though spent thy flame, in me the heat remaining;
I that have loved thee thus before thou fadest,
My faith shall wax when thou art in thy waning.
    The world shall find this miracle in me
That fire can burn when all the matter's spent;
Then what my faith hath been thy self shalt see,
And that thou wast unkind thou mayst repent.
      Thou mayst repent that thou hast scorned my tears,
      When winter snows upon thy golden hairs.

4

When winter snows upon thy golden hairs,
And frost of age hath nipped thy flowers near;
When dark shall seem thy day, that never clears,
And all lies withered that was held so dear:
    Then take this picture which I here present thee,
Limned with a pencil not all unworthy;
Here see the gifts that God and Nature lent thee;
Here read thy self, and what I suffered for thee.
    This may remain thy lasting monument
Which happily posterity may cherish;
These colours with thy fading are not spent;
These may remain when thou and I shall perish.
      If they remain, then thou shalt live thereby;
      They will remain, and so thou canst not die.

5

Thou canst not die whilst any zeal abound
In feeling hearts that can conceive these lines;
Though thou, a Laura, hast no Petrarch found,
In base attire yet clearly beauty shines.
    And I, though born within a colder clime,
Do feel mine inward heat as great, I know it;
He never had more faith, although more rhyme;
I love as well, though he could better show it.
    But I may add one feather to thy fame,
To help her flight throughout the fairest isle;
And if my pen could more enlarge thy name,
Then shouldst thou live in an immortal style.
    But though that Laura better limnèd be,
    Suffice, thou shalt be loved as well as she.

6

O be not grieved that these my papers should
Bewray unto the world how fair thou art,
Or that my wits have showed the best they could,
The chastest flame that ever warmèd heart.
    Think not, sweet Delia, this shall be thy shame;
My muse should sound thy praise with mournful warble;
How many live, the glory of whose name
Shall rest in ice, when thine is graved in marble.
    Thou mayst in after ages live esteemed,
Unburied in these lines, reserved in pureness;
These shall entomb those eyes, that have redeemed
Me from the vulgar, thee from all obscureness.
    Although my careful accents never moved thee,
    Yet count it no disgrace that I have loved thee.

7

Delia, these eyes that so admireth thine
Have seen those walls the which ambition reared
To check the world, how they entombed have lien
Within themselves, and on them ploughs have eared.
    Yet for all that, no barbarous hand attained
The spoil of fame deserved by virtuous men,
Whose glorious actions luckily hath gained
The eternal annals of a happy pen.
    Why then, though Delia fade, let that not move her,
Though time do spoil her of the fairest veil
That ever yet mortality did cover,
Which shall enstar the needle and the trail.
      That grace, that virtue, all that served t'-in-woman,
      Doth her unto eternity asummon.

8

Fair and lovely maid, look from the shore;
See thy Leander striving in these waves;
Poor soul forspent, whose force can do no more,
Now send forth hopes, for now calm pity saves;
    And waft him to thee with those lovely eyes,
A happy convoy to a holy land;
Now show thy power, and where thy virtue lies;
To save thine own, stretch out the fairest hand.
    Stretch out the fairest hand, a pledge of peace;
That hand that darts so right and never misses;
I'll not revenge old wrongs, my wrath shall cease;
For that which gave me wounds, I'll give it kisses.
      Once let the ocean of my cares find shore,
      That thou be pleased, and I may sigh no more.

9

My Cynthia hath the waters of mine eyes,
The ready handmaids on her grace attending,
That never fall to ebb, nor ever dries,
For to their flow she never grants an ending.
    The ocean never did attend more duly
Upon his sovereign's course, the night's pale queen,
Nor paid the impost of his waves more truly
Than mine to her in truth have ever been.
    Yet nought the rock of that hard heart can move,
Where beat these tears with zeal, and fury driveth;
And yet I rather languish in her love
Than I would joy the fairest she that liveth.
      I doubt to find such pleasure in my gaining
      As now I taste in compass of complaining.

10

Beauty, sweet love, is like the morning dew,
Whose short refresh upon the tender green
Cheers for a time, but till the sun doth shew,
And straight 'tis gone as it had never been.
    Soon doth it fade, that makes the fairest flourish;
Short is the glory of the blushing rose;
The hue which thou so carefully dost nourish,
Yet which at length thou must be forced to lose.
    When thou surcharged with burthen of thy years
Shalt bend thy wrinkles homeward to the earth;
When time hath made a passport for thy fears,
Dated in age, the calends of our death—
      But ah, no more; this hath been often told,
      And women grieve to think they must be old.

11

Care-charmer sleep, son of the sable night,
Brother to death, in silent darkness born,
Relieve my languish and restore the light,
With dark forgetting of my cares return:
    And let the day be time enough to mourn
The shipwrack of my ill-adventured youth;
Let waking eyes suffice to wail their scorn,
Without the torment of the night's untruth.
    Cease dreams, the imagery of our day desires,
To model forth the passions of the morrow;
Never let rising sun approve you liars,
To add more grief to aggravate my sorrow.
      Still let me sleep, embracing clouds in vain,
      And never wake to feel the day's disdain.

12

Let others sing of knights and paladins
In agèd accents and untimely words,
Paint shadows in imaginary lines,
Which well the reach of their high wits records;
    But I must sing of thee, and those fair eyes
Authentic shall my verse in time to come,
When yet th'unborn shall say, 'lo where she lies,
Whose beauty made him speak, that else was dumb'.
    These are the arks, the trophies I erect,
That fortify thy name against old age;
And these thy sacred virtues must protect
Against the dark, and time's consuming rage.
      Though th'error of my youth they shall discover,
      Suffice they show I lived and was thy lover.

MICHAEL DRAYTON (1563–1631)

Idea

I

Into these loves who but for passion looks,
At this first sight here let him lay them by,
And seek elsewhere, in turning other books,
Which better may his labour satisfy.
No far-fetched sigh shall ever wound my breast;
Love from mine eye a tear shall never wring;
Nor in 'ah me's' my whining sonnets dressed;
A libertine, fantastically I sing.
My verse is the true image of my mind,
Ever in motion, still desiring change;
And, as thus to variety inclined,
So in all humours sportively I range:
    My muse is rightly of the English strain,
    That cannot long one fashion entertain.

2

Like an adventurous seafarer am I
Who hath some long and dangerous voyage been,
And, called to tell of his discovery,
How far he sailed, what countries he had seen,
Proceeding from the port whence he put forth
Shows by his compass how his course he steered,
When east, when west, when south, and when by north,
As how the pole to every place was reared;
What capes he doubled, of what continent,
The gulfs and straits that strangely he had passed,
Where most becalmed, where with foul weather spent,
And on what rocks in peril to be cast:
    Thus in my love time calls me to relate
    My tedious travels and oft-varying fate.

3

My heart was slain, and none but you and I:
Who should I think the murder should commit?
Since, but yourself, there was no creature by
But only I, guiltless of murdering it.
It slew itself? the verdict on the view
Do quit the dead, and me not accessary:
Well, well, I fear it will be proved by you,
The evidence so great a proof doth carry.
But oh, see, see! We need enquire no further:
Upon your lips the scarlet drops are found;
And in your eye, the boy that did the murther,
Your cheeks yet pale, since first he gave the wound.
    By this I see, however things be past,
    Yet heaven will still have murder out at last.

4

Nothing but No and Ay, and Ay and No:
How falls it out so strangely you reply?
I tell ye, fair, I'll not be answered so
With this affirming No, denying Ay.
I say 'I love'; you slightly answer 'Ay';
I say 'You love'; you pule me out a 'No';
I say 'I die'; you echo me with 'Ay';
'Save me,' I cry; you sigh me out a 'No'.
Must woe and I have naught but No and Ay?
No I am I, if I no more can have;
Answer no more, with silence make reply,
And let me take myself what I do crave:
    Let No and Ay with I and you be so;
    Then answer 'No and I', and 'I and No'.

5

How many paltry, foolish, painted things,
That now in coaches trouble every street,
Shall be forgotten, whom no poet sings,
Ere they be well wrapped in their winding sheet,
Where I to thee eternity shall give
When nothing else remaineth of these days;
And queens hereafter shall be glad to live
Upon the alms of thy superfluous praise.
Virgins and matrons, reading these my rhymes,
Shall be so much delighted with thy story
That they shall grieve they lived not in these times
To have seen thee, their sex's only glory.
  So shalt thou fly above the vulgar throng,
    Still to survive in my immortal song.

6

You not alone when you are still alone;
O God, from you that I could private be!
Since you one were, I never since was one,
Since you in me, my self since out of me;
Transported from myself into your being,
Though either distant, present yet to either,
Senseless with too much joy, each other seeing,
And only absent when we are together.
Give me my self, and take your self again;
Devise some means but how I may forsake you;
So much is mine that doth with you remain,
That taking what is mine, with me I take you.
  You do bewitch me; O, that I could fly
    From myself you, or from your own self I!

7

Since to obtain thee nothing me will stead,
I have a medicine that shall cure my love:
The powder of her heart, dried, when she is dead,
That gold nor honour ne'er had power to move;
Mixed with her tears, that ne'er her true-love crossed,
Nor at fifteen ne'er longed to be a bride;
Boiled with her sighs, in giving up the ghost,
That for her late deceasèd husband died.
Into the same then let a woman breathe
That, being chid, did never word reply;
With one thrice-married's prayers, that did bequeath
A legacy to stale virginity.
    If this receipt have not the power to win me,
    Little I'll say, but think the devil's in me.

8

Stay, speedy Time; behold, before thou pass
From age to age, what thou hast sought to see:
One in whom all the excellencies be,
In whom heaven looks itself as in a glass.
Time, look thou too in this tralucent glass,
And thy youth past in this pure mirror see,
As the world's beauty in his infancy,
What it was then, and thou before it was.
Pass on, and to posterity tell this;
Yet see thou tell but truly what hath been:
Say to our nephews that thou once hast seen
In perfect human shape all heavenly bliss;
    And bid them mourn, nay more, despair with thee,
    That she is gone, her like again to see.

9

You cannot love, my pretty heart; and why?
There was a time you told me that you would;
But now again you will the same deny;
If it might please you, would to God you could!
What, will you hate? Nay, that you will not neither.
Nor love nor hate; how then? What will you do?
What, will you keep a mean, then, betwixt either?
Or will you love me and yet hate me too?
Yet serves not this: what next, what other shift?
You will and will not; what a coil is here!
I see your craft; now I perceive your drift;
And all this while I was mistaken there.
    Your love and hate is this, I now do prove you:
    You love in hate, by hate to make me love you.

10

Love, banished heaven, in earth was held in scorn,
Wandering abroad in need and beggary;
And wanting friends, though of a goddess born,
Yet craved the alms of such as passèd by.
I, like a man devout and charitable,
Clothèd the naked, lodged this wandering guest,
With sighs and tears still furnishing his table
With what might make the miserable blest.
But this ungrateful, for my good desert
Enticed my thoughts against me to conspire,
Who gave consent to steal away my heart,
And set my breast, his lodging, on a fire.
    Well, well, my friends; when beggars grow thus bold,
    No marvel, then, though charity grow cold.

11

I hear some say, 'This man is not in love.
Who? Can he love? A likely thing!' they say;
'Read but his verse, and it will easily prove'.
O, judge not rashly, gentle sir, I pray.
Because I loosely trifle in this sort,
As one that fain his sorrows would beguile,
You now suppose me all this time in sport,
And please yourself with this conceit the while.
Ye shallow censures, sometime see ye not
In greatest perils some men pleasant be,
Where fame by death is only to be got,
They resolute. So stands the case with me.
    Where other men in depth of passion cry,
      I laugh at fortune, as in jest to die.

12

Calling to mind since first my love begun,
Th' incertain times oft varying in their course,
How things still unexpectedly have run,
As't please the fates, by their resistless force,
Lastly, mine eyes amazedly have seen
Essex' great fall, Tyrone his peace to gain,
The quiet end of that long-living Queen,
This King's fair entrance, and our peace with Spain,
We and the Dutch at length ourselves to sever;
Thus the world doth, and evermore shall reel:
Yet to my goddess am I constant ever,
Howe'er blind fortune turn her giddy wheel.
    Though heaven and earth prove both to me untrue,
      Yet am I still inviolate to you.

13

As Love and I, late harboured in one inn,
With proverbs thus each other entertain,
'In love there is no lack,' thus I begin;
'Fair words make fools,' replieth he again.
'Who spares to speak doth spare to speed', quoth I;
'As well,' saith he, 'too forward as too slow';
'Fortune assists the boldest,' I reply;
'A hasty man,' quoth he, 'ne'er wanted woe';
'Labour is light where love,' quoth I, 'doth pay';
Saith he, 'Light burden's heavy if far borne';
Quoth I, 'The main lost, cast the by away';
'You have spun a fine thread,' he replies in scorn.
   And having thus a while each other thwarted,
     Fools as we met, so fools again we parted.

14

Since there's no help, come, let us kiss and part.
Nay, I have done; you get no more of me;
And I am glad, yea, glad with all my heart,
That thus so cleanly I myself can free.
Shake hands for ever, cancel all our vows,
And when we meet at any time again,
Be it not seen in either of our brows
That we one jot of former love retain.
Now at the last gasp of love's latest breath,
When, his pulse failing, passion speechless lies,
When faith is kneeling by his bed of death,
And innocence is closing up his eyes:
   Now, if thou wouldst, when all have given him over,
     From death to life thou might'st him yet recover.

WILLIAM SHAKESPEARE (1564–1616)

Sonnets

I (II)

When forty winters shall besiege thy brow
And dig deep trenches in thy beauty's field,
Thy youth's proud livery, so gazed on now,
Will be a tattered weed of small worth held.
Then, being asked where all thy beauty lies,
Where all the treasure of thy lusty days,
To say, within thine own deep sunken eyes,
Were an all-eating shame and thriftless praise.
How much more praise deserved thy beauty's use
If thou couldst answer, 'This fair child of mine
Shall sum my count, and make my old excuse',
Proving his beauty by succession thine.
 This were to be new made when thou art old,
 And see thy blood warm when thou feel'st it cold.

2 (V)

Those hours that with gentle work did frame
The lovely gaze where every eye doth dwell
Will play the tyrants to the very same,
And that unfair which fairly doth excel.
For never-resting time leads summer on
To hideous winter and confounds him there,
Sap checked with frost and lusty leaves quite gone,
Beauty o'ersnowed, and bareness everywhere.
Then, were not summer's distillation left
A liquid prisoner pent in walls of glass,
Beauty's effect with beauty were bereft;
Nor it, nor no remembrance what it was.
 But flowers distilled, though they with winter meet,
 Leese but their show; their substance still lives sweet.

3 (VII)

Lo, in the orient when the gracious light
Lifts up his burning head, each under eye
Doth homage to his new-appearing sight,
Serving with looks his sacred majesty;
And having climbed the steep-up heavenly hill,
Resembling strong youth in his middle age,
Yet mortal looks adore his beauty still,
Attending on his golden pilgrimage;
But when from highmost pitch with weary car
Like feeble age he reeleth from the day,
The eyes, 'fore duteous, now converted are
From his low tract, and look another way.
    So thou, thyself outgoing in thy noon,
      Unlooked on diest, unless thou get a son.

4 (XII)

When I do count the clock that tells the time,
And see the brave day sunk in hideous night;
When I behold the violet past prime,
And sable curls all silvered o'er with white;
When lofty trees I see barren of leaves,
Which erst from heat did canopy the herd,
And summer's green all girded up in sheaves,
Borne on the bier with white and bristly beard;
Then of thy beauty do I question make
That thou among the wastes of time must go,
Since sweets and beauties do themselves forsake,
And die as fast as they see others grow;
    And nothing 'gainst time's scythe can make defence
      Save breed, to brave him when he takes thee hence.

5 (XIII)

O that you were yourself: but, love, you are
No longer yours than you yourself here live;
Against this coming end you should prepare,
And your sweet semblance to some other give.
So should that beauty which you hold in lease
Find no determination; then you were
Yourself again after your self's decease,
When your sweet issue your sweet form should bear.
Who lets so fair a house fall to decay,
Which husbandry in honour might uphold
Against the stormy gusts of winter's day,
And barren rage of death's eternal cold?
    O, none but unthrifts, dear my love, you know:
    You had a father; let your son say so.

6 (XIV)

Not from the stars do I my judgment pluck,
And yet methinks I have astronomy;
But not to tell of good or evil luck,
Of plagues, of dearths, or seasons' quality;
Nor can I fortune to brief minutes tell,
Pointing to each his thunder, rain, and wind;
Or say with princes if it shall go well
By oft predict that I in heaven find.
But from thine eyes my knowledge I derive,
And, constant stars, in them I read such art
As truth and beauty shall together thrive
If from thyself to store thou wouldst convert.
    Or else of thee this I prognosticate:
    Thy end is truth's and beauty's doom and date.

7 (xv)

When I consider everything that grows
Holds in perfection but a little moment;
That this huge stage presenteth naught but shows
Whereon the stars in secret influence comment;
When I perceive that men as plants increase,
Cheered and checked even by the selfsame sky,
Vaunt in their youthful sap, at height decrease,
And wear their brave state out of memory;
Then the conceit of this inconstant stay
Sets you most rich in youth before my sight,
Where wasteful Time debateth with Decay
To change your day of youth to sullied night;
   And all in war with time for love of you,
   As he takes from you, I engraft you new.

8 (xvii)

Who will believe my verse in time to come,
If it were filled with your most high deserts?
Though yet, heaven knows, it is but as a tomb
Which hides your life, and shows not half your parts.
If I could write the beauty of your eyes,
And in fresh numbers number all your graces,
The age to come would say, 'This poet lies;
Such heavenly touches ne'er touched earthly faces'.
So should my papers, yellowed with their age,
Be scorned, like old men of less truth than tongue,
And your true rights be termed a poet's rage,
And stretchèd metre of an antique song.
   But were some child of yours alive that time,
   You should live twice: in it, and in my rhyme.

9 (XVIII)

Shall I compare thee to a summer's day?
Thou art more lovely and more temperate.
Rough winds do shake the darling buds of May,
And summer's lease hath all too short a date.
Sometime too hot the eye of heaven shines,
And often is his gold complexion dimmed;
And every fair from fair some time declines,
By chance, or nature's changing course, untrimmed.
But thy eternal summer shall not fade,
Nor lose possession of that fair thou ow'st;
Nor shall Death brag thou wanderest in his shade,
When in eternal lines to time thou grow'st.
    So long as men can breathe, or eyes can see,
    So long lives this, and this gives life to thee.

10 (XIX)

Devouring Time, blunt thou the lion's paws,
And make the earth devour her own sweet brood;
Pluck the keen teeth from the fierce tiger's jaws,
And burn the long-lived phoenix in her blood;
Make glad and sorry seasons as thou fleets,
And do whate'er thou wilt, swift-footed Time,
To the wide world and all her fading sweets;
But I forbid thee one most heinous crime:
O, carve not with thy hours my love's fair brow,
Nor draw no lines there with thine antic pen;
Him in thy course untainted do allow
For beauty's pattern to succeeding men.
    Yet do thy worst, old Time: despite thy wrong,
    My love shall in my verse ever live young.

11 (XX)

A woman's face, with Nature's own hand painted,
Hast thou, the master mistress of my passion;
A woman's gentle heart, but not acquainted
With shifting change, as is false woman's fashion;
An eye more bright than theirs, less false in rolling,
Gilding the object whereupon it gazeth;
A man in hue, all hues in his controlling,
Which steals men's eyes and women's souls amazeth.
And for a woman wert thou first created,
Till Nature as she wrought thee fell a-doting,
And by addition me of thee defeated
By adding one thing to my purpose nothing.
   But since she pricked thee out for women's pleasure,
   Mine be thy love, and thy love's use their treasure.

12 (XXVII)

Weary with toil, I haste me to my bed,
The dear repose for limbs with travel tired;
But then begins a journey in my head
To work my mind when body's work's expired;
For then my thoughts, from far where I abide,
Intend a zealous pilgrimage to thee,
And keep my drooping eyelids open wide,
Looking on darkness which the blind do see;
Save that my soul's imaginary sight
Presents thy shadow to my sightless view,
Which, like a jewel hung in ghastly night,
Makes black night beauteous and her old face new.
   Lo, thus by day my limbs, by night my mind,
   For thee and for myself no quiet find.

13 (XXIX)

When in disgrace with fortune and men's eyes
I all alone beweep my outcast state,
And trouble deaf heaven with my bootless cries,
And look upon myself, and curse my fate;
Wishing me like to one more rich in hope,
Featured like him, like him with friends possessed,
Desiring this man's art, and that man's scope,
With what I most enjoy contented least;
Yet in these thoughts myself almost despising,
Haply I think on thee, and then my state
Like to the lark at break of day arising
For sullen earth, sings hymns at heaven's gate:
　　For thy sweet love remembered such wealth brings
　　That then I scorn to change my state with kings.

14 (XXX)

When to the sessions of sweet silent thought
I summon up remembrance of things past,
I sigh the lack of many a thing I sought,
And with old woes new wail my dear time's waste.
Then can I drown an eye, unused to flow,
For precious friends hid in death's dateless night,
And weep afresh love's long since cancelled woe,
And moan the expense of many a vanished sight.
Then can I grieve at grievances foregone,
And heavily from woe to woe tell o'er
The sad account of fore-bemoanèd moan,
Which I new pay as if not paid before.
　　But if the while I think on thee, dear friend,
　　All losses are restored, and sorrows end.

15 (XXXIII)

Full many a glorious morning have I seen
Flatter the mountain-tops with sovereign eye,
Kissing with golden face the meadows green,
Gilding pale streams with heavenly alchemy;
Anon permit the basest clouds to ride
With ugly rack on his celestial face,
And from the forlorn world his visage hide,
Stealing unseen to west with this disgrace.
Even so my Sun one early morn did shine
With all-triumphant splendour on my brow;
But out, alack, he was but one hour mine;
The region cloud hath masked him from me now.
   Yet him for this my love no whit disdaineth;
    Suns of the world may stain when heaven's sun staineth.

16 (XXXIV)

Why didst thou promise such a beauteous day,
And make me travel forth without my cloak,
To let base clouds o'ertake me in my way,
Hiding thy bravery in their rotten smoke?
'Tis not enough that through the cloud thou break
To dry the rain on my storm-beaten face,
For no man well of such a salve can speak
That heals the wound, and cures not the disgrace.
Nor can thy shame give physic to my grief;
Though thou repent, yet I have still the loss;
Th'offender's sorrow lends but weak relief
To him that bears the strong offence's cross.
   Ah, but those tears are pearl which my love sheeds,
    And they are rich, and ransom all ill deeds.

17 (XXXV)

No more be grieved at that which thou hast done;
Roses have thorns, and silver fountains mud;
Clouds and eclipses stain both moon and sun,
And loathsome canker lives in sweetest bud.
All men make faults, and even I in this,
Authorizing thy trespass with compare,
Myself corrupting, salving thy amiss,
Excusing thy sins more than their sins are:
For to thy sensual fault I bring in sense;
Thy adverse party is thy advocate;
And 'gainst myself a lawful plea commence:
Such civil war is in my love and hate
    That I an accessary needs must be
    To that sweet thief which sourly robs from me.

18 (XXXVI)

Let me confess that we two must be twain,
Although our undivided loves are one;
So shall those blots that do with me remain,
Without thy help by me be borne alone.
In our two loves there is but one respect,
Though in our lives a separable spite,
Which though it alter not love's sole effect,
Yet doth it steal sweet hours from love's delight.
I may not evermore acknowledge thee
Lest my bewailèd guilt should do thee shame,
Nor thou with public kindness honour me,
Unless thou take that honour from thy name.
    But do not so; I love thee in such sort
    As, thou being mine, mine is thy good report.

19 (XLI)

Those pretty wrongs that liberty commits
When I am sometime absent from thy heart,
Thy beauty and thy years full well befits,
For still temptation follows where thou art.
Gentle thou art, and therefore to be won,
Beauteous thou art, therefore to be assailed;
And when a woman woos, what woman's son
Will sourly leave her till he have prevailed?
Ay me! But yet thou mightst my seat forbear,
And chide thy beauty and thy straying youth,
Who lead thee in their riot even there
Where thou art forced to break a twofold truth:
  Hers, by thy beauty tempting her to thee,
  Thine, by thy beauty being false to me.

20 (XLIX)

Against that time, if ever that time come,
When I shall see thee frown on my defects,
Whenas thy love hath cast his utmost sum,
Called to that audit by advised respects;
Against that time when thou shalt strangely pass
And scarcely greet me with that sun, thine eye,
When love, converted from the thing it was,
Shall reasons find of settled gravity;
Against that time do I ensconce me here
Within the knowledge of mine own desert,
And this my hand against myself uprear,
To guard the lawful reasons on thy part.
  To leave poor me thou hast the strength of laws,
  Since why to love I can allege no cause.

21 (LII)

So am I as the rich, whose blessèd key
Can bring him to his sweet up-lockèd treasure,
The which he will not every hour survey
For blunting the fine point of seldom pleasure.
Therefore are feasts so solemn and so rare,
Since seldom coming, in the long year set,
Like stones of worth they thinly placèd are,
Or captain jewels in the carcanet.
So is the time that keeps you as my chest,
Or as the wardrobe which the robe doth hide,
To make some special instant special blest
By new unfolding his imprisoned pride.
    Blessèd are you, whose worthiness gives scope
    Being had, to triumph, being lacked, to hope.

22 (LV)

Not marble nor the gilded monuments
Of princes shall outlive this powerful rhyme;
But you shall shine more bright in these contents
Then unswept stone, besmeared with sluttish time.
When wasteful war shall statues overturn,
And broils root out the work of masonry,
Nor Mars his sword nor war's quick fire shall burn
The living record of your memory.
'Gainst death and all-oblivious enmity
Shall you pace forth; your praise shall still find room
Even in the eyes of all posterity
That wear this world out to the ending doom.
    So, till the judgment that your self arise,
    You live in this, and dwell in lovers' eyes.

23 (LX)

Like as the waves make towards the pebbled shore,
So do our minutes hasten to their end;
Each changing place with that which goes before,
In sequent toil all forwards do contend.
Nativity, once in the main of light,
Crawls to maturity, wherewith being crowned,
Crooked eclipses 'gainst his glory fight,
And Time that gave doth now his gift confound.
Time doth transfix the flourish set on youth,
And delves the parallels in beauty's brow,
Feeds on the rarities of nature's truth,
And nothing stands but for his scythe to mow.
   And yet to times in hope my verse shall stand,
   Praising thy worth, despite his cruel hand.

24 (LXIV)

When I have seen by Time's fell hand defaced
The rich proud cost of outworn buried age;
When sometime lofty towers I see down-rased,
And brass eternal slave to mortal rage;
When I have seen the hungry ocean gain
Advantage on the kingdom of the shore,
And the firm soil win of the watery main,
Increasing store with loss, and loss with store;
When I have seen such interchange of state,
Or state itself confounded to decay;
Ruin hath taught me thus to ruminate
That Time will come and take my love away.
   This thought is as a death, which cannot choose
   But weep to have that which it fears to lose.

25 (LXV)

Since brass, nor stone, nor earth, nor boundless sea,
But sad mortality o'ersways their power,
How with this rage shall beauty hold a plea,
Whose action is no stronger than a flower?
O how shall summer's honey breath hold out
Against the wrackful siege of battering days,
When rocks impregnable are not so stout,
Nor gates of steel so strong, but Time decays?
O fearful meditation! Where, alack,
Shall Time's best jewel from Time's chest lie hid?
Or what strong hand can hold his swift foot back,
Or who his spoil of beauty can forbid?
   O none, unless this miracle have might,
   That in black ink my love may still shine bright.

26 (LXXI)

No longer mourn for me when I am dead
Than you shall hear the surly sullen bell
Give warning to the world that I am fled
From this vile world, with vilest worms to dwell.
Nay, if you read this line, remember not
The hand that writ it, for I love you so
That I in your sweet thoughts would be forgot,
If thinking on me then should make you woe.
Or if, I say, you look upon this verse
When I perhaps compounded am with clay,
Do not so much as my poor name rehearse,
But let your love even with my life decay.
   Lest the wise world should look into your moan,
   And mock you with me after I am gone.

27 (LXXIII)

That time of year thou mayst in me behold
When yellow leaves, or none, or few, do hang
Upon those boughs which shake against the cold,
Bare ruined choirs, where late the sweet birds sang.
In me thou seest the twilight of such day
As after sunset fadeth in the west,
Which by and by black night doth take away,
Death's second self, that seals up all in rest.
In me thou seest the glowing of such fire
That in the ashes of his youth doth lie,
As the death-bed whereon it must expire,
Consumed with that which it was nourished by.
  This thou perceiv'st, which makes thy love more strong
  To love that well which thou must leave ere long.

28 (LXXIV)

But be contented when that fell arrest
Without all bail shall carry me away;
My life hath in this line some interest,
Which for memorial still with thee shall stay.
When thou reviewest this, thou dost review
The very part was consecrate to thee;
The earth can have but earth which is his due;
My spirit is thine, the better part of me.
So then thou hast but lost the dregs of life,
The prey of worms, my body being dead;
The coward conquest of a wretch's knife,
Too base of thee to be rememberèd.
  The worth of that is that which it contains,
  And that is this, and this with thee remains.

29 (LXXXVI)

Was it the proud full sail of his great verse,
Bound for the prize of all-too-precious you,
That did my ripe thoughts in my brain inhearse,
Making their tomb the womb wherein they grew?
Was it his spirit, by spirits taught to write
Above a mortal pitch, that struck me dead?
No, neither he, nor his compeers by night
Giving him aid, my verse astonishèd:
He, nor that affable familiar ghost
Which nightly gulls him with intelligence,
As victors of my silence cannot boast:
I was not sick of any fear from thence.
   But when your countenance filled up his line,
   Then lacked I matter; that enfeebled mine.

30 (LXXXVII)

Farewell, thou art too dear for my possessing;
And like enough thou know'st thy estimate.
The charter of thy worth gives thee releasing;
My bonds in thee are all determinate.
For how do I hold thee but by thy granting?
And for that riches where is my deserving?
The cause of this fair gift in me is wanting,
And so my patent back again is swerving.
Thy self thou gav'st, thy own worth then not knowing,
Or me to whom thou gav'st it else mistaking;
So thy great gift, upon misprision growing,
Comes home again, on better judgment making.
   Thus have I had thee, as a dream doth flatter;
   In sleep a king, but waking, no such matter.

31 (XCIV)

They that have power to hurt and will do none,
That do not do the thing they most do show,
Who, moving others, are themselves as stone,
Unmovèd, cold, and to temptation slow:
They rightly do inherit heaven's graces,
And husband nature's riches from expense;
They are the lords and owners of their faces,
Others, but stewards of their excellence.
The summer's flower is to the summer sweet
Though to itself it only live and die;
But if that flower with base infection meet,
The basest weed outbraves his dignity.
    For sweetest things turn sourest by their deeds:
    Lilies that fester smell far worse than weeds.

32 (CIV)

To me, fair friend, you never can be old;
For as you were when first your eye I eyed,
Such seems your beauty still. Three winters' cold
Have from the forests shook three summers' pride,
Three beauteous springs to yellow autumn turned,
In process of the seasons have I seen;
Three April perfumes in three hot Junes burned,
Since first I saw you fresh, which yet are green.
Ah yet doth beauty like a dial hand
Steal from his figure, and no pace perceived;
So your sweet hue, which methinks still doth stand,
Hath motion, and mine eye may be deceived.
    For fear of which, hear this, thou age unbred:
    Ere you were born was beauty's summer dead.

33 (CVI)

When in the chronicle of wasted time
I see descriptions of the fairest wights,
And beauty making beautiful old rhyme
In praise of ladies dead and lovely knights,
Then, in the blazon of sweet beauty's best,
Of hand, of foot, of lip, of eye, of brow,
I see their antique pen would have expressed
Even such a beauty as you master now.
So all their praises are but prophecies
Of this our time, all you prefiguring;
And, for they looked but with divining eyes,
They had not still enough your praise to sing;
   For we which now behold these present days
   Have eyes to wonder, but lack tongues to praise.

34 (CVII)

Not mine own fears, nor the prophetic soul
Of the wide world dreaming on things to come
Can yet the lease of my true love control,
Supposed as forfeit to a confined doom.
The mortal moon hath her eclipse endured,
And the sad augurs mock their own presage;
Incertainties now crown themselves assured,
And peace proclaims olives of endless age.
Now with the drops of this most balmy time
My love looks fresh, and Death to me subscribes,
Since spite of him I'll live in this poor rhyme,
While he insults o'er dull and speechless tribes.
   And thou in this shalt find thy monument
   When tyrants' crests and tombs of brass are spent.

35 (CVIII)

What's in the brain that ink may character
Which hath not figured to thee my true spirit?
What's new to speak, what now to register,
That may express my love or thy dear merit?
Nothing, sweet boy; but yet, like prayers divine,
I must each day say o'er the very same,
Counting no old thing old, thou mine, I thine,
Even as when first I hallowed thy fair name.
So that eternal love in love's fresh case
Weighs not the dust and injury of age,
Nor gives to necessary wrinkles place,
But makes eternity for aye his page;
    Finding the first conceit of love there bred
    Where time and outward form would show it dead.

36 (CX)

Alas, 'tis true I have gone here and there,
And made myself a motley to the view,
Gored mine own thoughts, sold cheap what is most dear,
Made old offences of affections new.
Most true it is that I have looked on truth
Askance and strangely; but, by all above,
These blenches gave my heart another youth,
And worse essays proved thee my best of love.
Now all is done, have what shall have no end;
Mine appetite I never more will grind
On newer proof to try an older friend,
A god in love, to whom I am confined.
    Then give me welcome, next my heaven the best,
    Even to thy pure and most most loving breast.

37 (CXI)

O for my sake do you with Fortune chide,
The guilty goddess of my harmful deeds,
That did not better for my life provide
Than public means, which public manners breeds.
Thence comes it that my name receives a brand,
And almost thence my nature is subdued
To what it works in, like the dyer's hand;
Pity me then, and wish I were renewed;
Whilst like a willing patient, I will drink
Potions of eisel 'gainst my strong infection;
No bitterness that I will bitter think,
Nor double penance, to correct correction.
    Pity me then, dear friend, and I assure ye
    Even that your pity is enough to cure me.

38 (CXV)

Those lines that I before have writ do lie,
Even those that said I could not love you dearer;
Yet then my judgment knew no reason why
My most full flame should afterwards burn clearer.
But reckoning Time, whose millioned accidents
Creep in 'twixt vows and change decrees of kings,
Tan sacred beauty, blunt the sharp'st intents,
Divert strong minds to th' course of altering things,
Alas, why, fearing of Time's tyranny,
Might I not then say, 'Now I love you best',
When I was certain o'er incertainty,
Crowning the present, doubting of the rest?
    Love is a babe; then might I not say so
    To give full growth to that which still doth grow?

39 (CXVI)

Let me not to the marriage of true minds
Admit impediments: love is not love
Which alters when it alteration finds,
Or bends with the remover to remove.
O no, it is an ever-fixèd mark,
That looks on tempests and is never shaken;
It is the star to every wandering bark,
Whose worth's unknown, although his height be taken.
Love's not Time's fool, though rosy lips and cheeks
Within his bending sickle's compass come;
Love alters not with his brief hours and weeks,
But bears it out even to the edge of doom.
    If this be error, and upon me proved,
    I never writ, nor no man ever loved.

40 (CXIX)

What potions have I drunk of siren tears,
Distilled from limbecks foul as hell within,
Applying fears to hopes, and hopes to fears,
Still losing, when I saw myself to win!
What wretched errors hath my heart committed
Whilst it hath thought itself so blessèd never;
How have mine eyes out of their spheres been fitted
In the distraction of this madding fever!
O benefit of ill: now I find true
That better is by evil still made better;
And ruined love, when it is built anew,
Grows fairer than at first, more strong, far greater.
    So I return rebuked to my content,
    And gain by ills thrice more than I have spent.

41 (CXX)

That you were once unkind befriends me now,
And for that sorrow which I then did feel
Needs must I under my transgression bow,
Unless my nerves were brass or hammered steel.
For if you were by my unkindness shaken
As I by yours, y'have passed a hell of time;
And I, a tyrant, have no leisure taken
To weigh how once I suffered in your crime.
O, that our night of woe might have remembered
My deepest sense, how hard true sorrow hits,
And soon to you, as you to me, then tendered
The humble salve which wounded bosoms fits!
  But that your trespass now becomes a fee;
  Mine ransoms yours, and yours must ransom me.

42 (CXXIII)

No, Time, thou shalt not boast that I do change.
Thy pyramids built up with newer might
To me are nothing novel, nothing strange;
They are but dressings of a former sight.
Our dates are brief, and therefore we admire
What thou dost foist upon us that is old,
And rather make them born to our desire
Than think that we before have heard them told.
Thy registers and thee I both defy,
Not wondering at the present nor the past,
For thy records and what we see doth lie,
Made more or less by thy continual haste.
  This I do vow, and this shall ever be:
  I will be true, despite thy scythe and thee.

43 (CXXIV)

If my dear love were but the child of state,
It might for Fortune's bastard be unfathered,
As subject to Time's love, or to Time's hate,
Weeds among weeds, or flowers with flowers gathered.
No, it was builded far from accident;
It suffers not in smiling pomp, nor falls
Under the blow of thrallèd discontent
Whereto the inviting time our fashion calls.
It fears not Policy, that heretic,
Which works on leases of short-numbered hours,
But all alone stands hugely politic,
That it nor grows with heat nor drowns with showers.
  To this I witness call the fools of time,
    Which die for goodness, who have lived for crime.

44 (CXXVI)

O thou, my lovely boy, who in thy power
Dost hold Time's fickle glass, his sickle Hour;
Who hast by waning grown, and therein show'st
Thy lovers withering as thy sweet self grow'st:
If Nature, sovereign mistress over wrack,
As thou goest onwards, still will pluck thee back,
She keeps thee to this purpose, that her skill
May Time disgrace, and wretched Minute kill.
Yet fear her, O thou minion of her pleasure:
She may detain, but not still keep, her treasure.
Her audit, though delayed, answered must be,
And her quietus is to render thee.

45 (CXXVII)

In the old age black was not counted fair,
Or if it were, it bore not beauty's name;
But now is black Beauty's successive heir,
And Beauty slandered with a bastard shame;
For since each hand hath put on Nature's power,
Fairing the foul with Art's false borrowed face,
Sweet Beauty hath no name, no holy bower,
But is profaned, if not lives in disgrace.
Therefore my mistress' eyes are raven black,
Her eyes so suited as they mourners seem
At such who, not born fair, no beauty lack,
Slandering creation with a false esteem.
  Yet so they mourn becoming of their woe,
  That every tongue says Beauty should be so.

46 (CXXVIII)

How oft when thou, my music, music play'st
Upon that blessèd wood whose motion sounds
With thy sweet fingers, when thou gently sway'st
The wiry concord that mine ear confounds,
Do I envy those jacks that nimble leap
To kiss the tender inward of thy hand,
Whilst my poor lips, which should that harvest reap,
At the wood's boldness by thee blushing stand!
To be so tickled, they would change their state
And situation with those dancing chips
O'er whom thy fingers walk with gentle gait,
Making dead wood more blest than living lips.
  Since saucy jacks so happy are in this,
  Give them thy fingers, me thy lips to kiss.

47 (CXXIX)

The expense of spirit in a waste of shame
Is lust in action; and till action, lust
Is perjured, murderous, bloody, full of blame,
Savage, extreme, rude, cruel, not to trust;
Enjoyed no sooner but despisèd straight;
Past reason hunted, and no sooner had,
Past reason hated, as a swallowed bait,
On purpose laid to make the taker mad;
Mad in pursuit, and in possession so;
Had, having, and in quest to have, extreme;
A bliss in proof, and proved, a very woe;
Before, a joy proposed; behind, a dream.
  All this the world well knows; yet none knows well
  To shun the heaven that leads men to this hell.

48 (CXXX)

My mistress' eyes are nothing like the sun;
Coral is far more red than her lips' red;
If snow be white, why then her breasts are dun;
If hairs be wires, black wires grow on her head.
I have seen roses damasked, red and white,
But no such roses see I in her cheeks;
And in some perfumes is there more delight
Than in the breath that from my mistress reeks.
I love to hear her speak, yet well I know
That music hath a far more pleasing sound;
I grant I never saw a goddess go;
My mistress when she walks treads on the ground.
  And yet by heaven, I think my love as rare
  As any she belied with false compare.

49 (CXXXIII)

Beshrew that heart that makes my heart to groan
For that deep wound it gives my friend and me!
Is't not enough to torture me alone,
But slave to slavery my sweet'st friend must be?
Me from my self thy cruel eye hath taken,
And my next self thou harder hast engrossed;
Of him, my self, and thee, I am forsaken;
A torment thrice threefold thus to be crossed.
Prison my heart in thy steel bosom's ward,
But then my friend's heart let my poor heart bail;
Whoe'er keeps me, let my heart be his guard;
Thou canst not then use rigour in my jail.
    And yet thou wilt; for I being pent in thee,
    Perforce am thine, and all that is in me.

50 (CXXXVII)

Thou blind fool Love, what dost thou to mine eyes,
That they behold, and see not what they see?
They know what beauty is, see where it lies,
Yet what the best is, take the worst to be.
If eyes corrupt by over-partial looks
Be anchored in the bay where all men ride,
Why of eyes' falsehood hast thou forgèd hooks,
Whereto the judgment of my heart is tied?
Why should my heart think that a several plot,
Which my heart knows the wide world's common place?
Or mine eyes seeing this, say this is not,
To put fair truth upon so foul a face?
    In things right true my heart and eyes have erred,
    And to this false plague are they now transferred.

51 (CXXXVIII)

When my love swears that she is made of truth,
I do believe her, though I know she lies,
That she might think me some untutored youth,
Unlearnèd in the world's false subtleties.
Thus vainly thinking that she thinks me young,
Although she knows my days are past the best,
Simply I credit her false-speaking tongue;
On both sides thus is simple truth suppressed.
But wherefore says she not she is unjust?
And wherefore say not I that I am old?
O, love's best habit is in seeming trust,
And age in love loves not to have years told.
    Therefore I lie with her, and she with me,
    And in our faults by lies we flattered be.

52 (CXLIV)

Two loves I have of comfort and despair,
Which like two spirits do suggest me still;
The better angel is a man right fair,
The worser spirit a woman coloured ill.
To win me soon to hell, my female evil
Tempteth my better angel from my side,
And would corrupt my saint to be a devil,
Wooing his purity with her foul pride.
And whether that my angel be turned fiend
Suspect I may, yet not directly tell;
But being both from me, both to each friend,
I guess one angel in another's hell.
    Yet this shall I ne'er know, but live in doubt,
    Till my bad angel fire my good one out.

53 (CXLVI)

Poor soul, the centre of my sinful earth,
Foiled by these rebel powers that thee array,
Why dost thou pine within and suffer dearth,
Painting thy outward walls so costly gay?
Why so large cost, having so short a lease,
Dost thou upon thy fading mansion spend?
Shall worms, inheritors of this excess,
Eat up thy charge? Is this thy body's end?
Then soul, live thou upon thy servant's loss,
And let that pine to aggravate thy store;
Buy terms divine in selling hours of dross;
Within be fed, without be rich no more.
  So shalt thou feed on Death that feeds on men,
  And Death once dead, there's no more dying then.

54 (CXLVII)

My love is as a fever, longing still
For that which longer nurseth the disease;
Feeding on that which doth preserve the ill,
The uncertain sickly appetite to please.
My reason, the physician to my love,
Angry that his prescriptions are not kept,
Hath left me, and I desperate now approve
Desire is death, which physic did except.
Past cure I am, now reason is past care,
And frantic mad with evermore unrest;
My thoughts and my discourse as madmen's are,
At random from the truth, vainly expressed:
  For I have sworn thee fair, and thought thee bright,
  Who art as black as hell, as dark as night.

FULKE GREVILLE (1554–1628)

Caelica

1 (XXXVIII)

Caelica, I overnight was finely used,
Lodged in the midst of paradise, your heart:
Kind thoughts had charge I might not be refused,
Of every fruit and flower I had part.
But curious Knowledge, blown with busy flame,
The sweetest fruits had down in shadows hidden,
And, for it found mine eyes had seen the same,
I from my paradise was straight forbidden.
Where that cur, Rumour, runs in every place,
Barking with Care, begotten out of Fear,
And glassy Honour, Tender of Disgrace,
Stands Seraphin to see I come not there;
    While that fine soil, which all these joys did yield,
    By broken fence is proved a common field.

2 (XXXIX)

The pride of flesh by reach of human wit
Did purpose once to overreach the sky;
And where before God drowned the world for it,
Yet Babylon it built up, not to die.
God knew these fools how foolishly they wrought,
That destiny with policy would break;
Straight none could tell his fellow what he thought,
Their tongues were changed, and men not taught to speak.
So I, that heavenly peace would comprehend
In mortal seat of Caelica's fair heart,
To Babylon myself there did intend,
With natural kindness, and with passion's art:
    But when I thought myself of herself free,
    All's changed: she understands all men but me.

3 (LXXXV)

Love is the peace whereto all thoughts do strive,
Done and begun with all our powers in one:
The first and last in us that is alive,
End of the good, and therewith pleased alone.
Perfection's spirit, goodness of the mind,
Passèd through hope, desire, grief and fear,
A simple goodness in the flesh refined,
Which of the joys to come doth witness bear.
Constant, because it sees no cause to vary,
A quintessence of passions overthrown,
Raised above all that change of objects carry,
A nature by no other nature known:
    For glory's of eternity a frame,
    That by all bodies else obscures her name.

4 (C)

In night, when colours all to black are cast,
Direction lost, or gone down with the light,
The eye a watch to inward senses placed,
Not seeing, yet still having power of sight,
Gives vain alarums to the inward sense,
Where fear stirred up with witty tyranny
Confounds all powers, and thorough self-offence,
Doth forge and raise impossibility:
Such as in thick depriving darknesses
Proper reflections of the error be,
And images of self-confusednesses,
Which hurt imaginations only see;
    And from this nothing seen, tells news of devils
    Which but expressions be of inward evils.

5 (CII)

O false and treacherous probability,
Enemy of truth, and friend to wickedness,
With those blear eyes Opinion learns to see,
Truth's feeble party here, and barrenness:
When thou hast thus misled humanity,
And lost obedience in the pride of wit,
With reason dar'st thou judge the deity,
And in thy flesh make bold to fashion it.
Vain thought! The word of power a riddle is,
And, till the veils be rent, the flesh new born,
Reveals no wonders of that inward bliss,
Which, but where faith is, everywhere finds scorn.
  Who therefore censures God with fleshly sprite
  As well in time may wrap up infinite.

WILLIAM DRUMMOND OF HAWTHORNDEN
(1585–1649)

I

How that vast heaven entitled First is rolled;
If any other worlds beyond it lie;
And people living in eternity,
Or essence pure, that doth this All uphold:
What motion have those fixèd sparks of gold,
The wandering carbuncles which shine from high;
By sprites, or bodies, contrarways in sky
If they be turned, and mortal things behold:
How sun posts heaven about, how night's pale queen
With borrowed beams looks on this hanging round;
What cause fair Iris hath, and monsters seen
In air's large fields of light, and seas profound,
    Did hold my wandering thoughts, when thy sweet eye
    Bade me leave all, and only think on thee.

2

The learned Grecian, who did so excel
In knowledge passing sense, that he is named
Of all the after-worlds 'divine', doth tell
That at the time when first our souls are framed,
Ere in these mansions blind they come to dwell,
They live, bright rays of that Eternal Light,
And others see, know, love, in heaven's great height,
Not toiled with ought to reason doth rebel.
Most true it is; for straight at the first sight
My mind me told that in some other place
It elsewhere saw the Idea of that face,
And loved a love of heavenly pure delight.
    No wonder now I feel so fair a flame,
    Sith I her loved ere on this earth she came.

3

Now, while the night her sable veil hath spread,
And silently her resty coach doth roll,
Rousing with her from Tethys' azure bed
Those starry nymphs which dance about the Pole;
While Cynthia, in purest cypress cled,
The Latmian shepherd in a trance descries,
And whiles looks pale from height of all the skies,
Whiles dyes her beauties in a bashful red;
While Sleep in triumph closèd hath all eyes,
And birds and beasts a silence sweet do keep,
And Proteus' monstrous people in the deep
The winds and waves, hushed up, to rest entice:
   I wake, muse, weep; and who my heart hath slain
   See still before me to augment my pain.

4

Sleep, Silence' child, sweet father of soft rest,
Prince, whose approach peace to all shepherds brings,
Indifferent host to mortals and to kings,
Sole comforter of minds with grief oppressed:
Lo, by thy charming-rod all breathing things
Lie slumbering with forgetfulness possessed;
And yet o'er me to spread thy drowsy wings
Thou spares, alas, who cannot be thy guest.
Since I am thine, O come, but with that face
To inward light which thou art wont to show;
With fainèd solace ease a true-felt woe;
Or if, deaf god, thou do deny that grace,
   Come as thou wilt, and what thou wilt bequeath;
   I long to kiss the image of my death.

5

A passing glance, a lightning 'long the skies
That, ushering thunder, dies straight to our sight;
A spark, of contraries which doth arise,
Then drowns in the huge depths of day and night,
Is this small small called life, held in such price
Of blinded wights, who nothing judge aright;
Of Parthian shaft so swift is not the flight
As life, that wastes itself, and, living, dies.
O what is human greatness, valour, wit?
What fading beauty, riches, honour, praise?
To what doth serve in golden thrones to sit,
Thrall earth's vast round, triumphal arches raise?
  All is a dream, learn in this prince's fall,
  In whom, save death, nought mortal was at all.

6

Triumphing chariots, statues, crowns of bays,
Sky-threatening arches, the rewards of worth,
Works heavenly wise in sweet harmonious lays,
Which sprites divine unto the world set forth;
States, which ambitious minds with blood do raise
From frozen Tanais to sun-gilded Gange,
Gigantic frames, held wonders rarely strange,
Like spiders' webs are made the sport of days.
All only constant is in constant change;
What done is, is undone, and when undone,
Into some other fashion doth it range;
Thus goes the floating world beneath the moon.
  Wherefore, my mind, above time, motion, place,
  Thee raise, and steps unknown to nature trace.

7

That space, where raging waves do now divide
From the great continent our happy isle,
Was sometime land, and where tall ships do glide
Once with dear art the crooked plough did tile.
Once those fair bounds stretched out so far and wide,
Where towns, no, shires enwalled endear each mile,
Were all ignoble sea and marish vile
Where Proteus' flocks danced measures to the tide.
So age, transforming all, still forward runs;
No wonder though the earth doth change her face,
New manners, pleasures new, turn with new suns,
Locks now like gold grow to an hoary grace;
  Nay, mind's rare shape doth change; that lies despised
  Which was so dear of late and highly prized.

8

Thrice happy he who by some shady grove,
Far from the clamorous world, doth live his own;
Though solitary, who is not alone,
But doth converse with that eternal love.
O, how more sweet is birds' harmonious moan,
Or the hoarse sobbings of the widowed dove,
Than those smooth whisperings near a prince's throne,
Which good make doubtful, do the evil approve!
O, how more sweet is Zephyr's wholesome breath,
And sighs enbalmed which new-born flowers unfold,
Than that applause vain honour doth bequeath!
How sweet are streams to poison drunk in gold!
  The world is full of horrors, troubles, slights;
  Woods' harmless shades have only true delights.

9

Sweet bird, that sing'st away the early hours,
Of winters past or coming void of care,
Well pleasèd with delights which present are,
Fair seasons, budding sprays, sweet-smelling flowers:
To rocks, to springs, to rills, from leavy bowers,
Thou thy Creator's goodness dost declare,
And what dear gifts on thee He did not spare,
A stain to human sense in sin that lowers.
What soul can be so sick, which by thy songs,
Attired in sweetness, sweetly is not driven
Quite to forget earth's turmoils, spites, and wrongs,
And lift a reverend eye and thought to heaven?
    Sweet artless song-star, thou my mind dost raise
    To airs of spheres, yes, and to angels' lays.

10

As when it happeneth that some lovely town
Unto a barbarous besieger falls,
Who there by sword and flame himself instals,
And, cruel, it in tears and blood doth drown;
Her beauty spoiled, her citizens made thralls;
His spite yet so cannot her all throw down,
But that some statue, arch, fane of renown
Yet lurks unmaimed within her weeping walls.
So, after all the spoil, disgrace, and wrack
That Time, the World, and Death could bring combined,
Amidst that mass of ruins they did make
Safe and all scarless yet remains my mind.
    From this so high transcending rapture springs
    That I, all else defaced, not envy kings.

WILLIAM ALABASTER (1567–1640)

Personal Sonnets

I

My friends, whose kindness doth their judgments blind,
Know you, say they, the dangers where you run,
Which zeal hides from you, but compassion
Tells us? You feel the blow, the smart we find.
I know it well, and as I call to mind,
This is the bill: dearness, affection,
Friends, fortune, pleasure, fame, hope, life undone,
Want, prison, torment, death, shame—what behind?
Is then my sense transel'mented to steel,
That neither this, nor that, nor all, can feel,
Nor can it bend my mind, which theirs doth break?
Not so, nor so; for I am not insensate,
But feel a double grief, that for Christ's sake
I have no more to spend, nor have spent that.

2

Lord, I have left all and myself behind:
My state, my hopes, my strength, and present ease,
My unprovokèd studies' sweet disease,
And touch of nature and engrafted kind,
Whose cleaving twist doth distant tempers bind;
And gentle sense of kindness that doth praise
The earnest judgments, others' wills to please;
All and myself I leave, thy love to find.
O strike my heart with lightning from above,
That from one wound both fire and blood may spring;
Fire to transelement my soul to love,
And blood as oil to keep the fire burning;
That fire may draw forth blood, blood extend fire,
Desire possession, possession desire.

Divine Meditations

3

The night, the starless night of passion
From heaven began, on heaven beneath to fall,
When Christ did sound the onset martial,
A sacred hymn, upon his foes to run;
That with the fiery contemplation
Of love and joy, his soul and senses all
Surchargèd might not dread the bitter thrall
Of pain and grief and torments all in one.
Then since my holy vows have undertook
To take the portrait of Christ's death in me,
Then let my love with sonnets fill this book,
With hymns to give the onset as did he;
That thoughts inflamèd with such heavenly muse
The coldest ice of fire may not refuse.

4

Over the brook of Cedron Christ is gone,
To entertain the combat with his death,
Where David fled beforetime void of breath
To scape the treacheries of Absalon.
Go, let us follow him in passion,
Over this brook, this world that walloweth,
A stream of cares that drown our thoughts beneath,
And wash away all resolution.
Beyond the world he must be passèd clear,
That in the world for Christ will troubles bear:
Leave we, O leave we then this miry flood,
Friends, pleasures, and unfaithful good.
Now we are up, now down, but cannot stand;
We sink, we reel; Jesu, stretch forth thy hand.

5

Though all forsake thee, Lord, yet I will die;
For I have chainèd so my will to thine
That I have no will left my will to untwine,
But will abide with thee most willingly.
Though all forsake thee, Lord, yet cannot I;
For love hath wrought in me thy form divine
That thou art more my heart than heart is mine:
How can I then from myself, thyself, fly?
Thus thought Saint Peter, and thus thinking, fell;
And by his fall did warn us not to swell.
Yet still in love I say I would not fall,
And say in hope, I trust I never shall;
But cannot say in faith what might I do
To learn to say it, by hearing Christ say so.

6

Jesus is risen from the infernal mire:
But who art thou that say'st Jesus arose?
Such holy words are only fit for those
Whose souls with Christ above the heavens aspire.
But if thou hast not raisèd thy desire
From earth to heaven, but in the world dost close
Thy love which unto heaven thou shouldst dispose,
Say not that Christ is yet ascended higher,
But yet within thy heart he lieth dead,
And by the devil is impoisonèd.
Rejoice not then in vain of his ascent;
For as his glorious rise doth much augment
All good men's hopes, so unto those that tread
False paths, it is a dreadful argument.

7

The earth, which in delicious paradise
Did bud forth man like cedars stately tall,
From barren womb accursèd by the fall
Doth thrust forth man as thorns in armèd wise,
Darting the points of sin against the skies.
With those thorns plaited was Christ's coronal,
Which crowned him then with grief, but after all
In heaven shall crown him, crown themselves with glory.
For with the purple tincture of his blood,
Which out the furrows of his brows did rain,
He hath transformed us thorns from baser wood
To raise our nature and odórant strain,
That we, who with our thorny sins did wound him,
Hereafter should with roseal virtues crown him.

8

Eternity, the womb of things created,
The endless bottom of duration,
Whose half was always past, yet unbegun,
And half behind still coming unabated;
Whose thread conjoinèd, both unseparated,
Is time, which dated is by motion;
Eternity, whose real thoughts are one
With God, that is everness actuated:
O tie my soul unto this endless clew,
That I may overfathom fate and time
In all my actions which I do pursue,
And bound my thoughts in that unbounded clime:
For soul and thoughts, designs and acts, are evil,
That under compass of this life do level.

9

The first beginning of creation
Was God; the end thereof in man was set;
End and beginning were together met;
So God and man became one person.
Thus nature's circle as a ring doth run,
Christ is the pale within whose circulet
The seal of the divinity is knit,
Which seal doth stand the Godhead's ring upon.
So stand two rings upon one diamond;
The knot of both and either, where are met
Finite and infinite, more and one;
Alpha and Omega in that fair tablet
Wherein is drawn the angels' alphabet,
Jesus. If he were learnt, need more be known?

10

O wretched man, the knot of contraries,
In whom both heaven and earth doth move and rest,
Heaven of my mind, which with Christ's love is blest,
Death of my heart, which in dull languor lies!
Yet doth my moving will still circulize
My heaven about my earth with thoughts' unrest,
Where reason as a sun from east to west
Darteth his shining beams to melt this ice.
And now with fear it southward doth descend,
Now between both is equinoctial,
And now to joys it higher doth ascend,
And yet continues my sea glacial.
What shall I do, but pray to Christ the Son?
In earth as heaven, Lord, let thy will be done.

JOHN DONNE (1573–1631)

Holy Sonnets

I

As due by many titles I resign
Myself to thee, O God; first I was made
By thee, and for thee; and when I was decayed
Thy blood bought that the which before was thine.
I am thy son, made with thyself to shine,
Thy servant, whose pains thou hast still repaid,
Thy sheep, thine image, and, till I betrayed
Myself, a temple of thy Spirit divine.
Why doth the devil then usurp in me?
Why doth he steal, nay ravish, that's thy right?
Except thou rise and for thine own work fight,
Oh, I shall soon despair, when I do see
That thou lov'st mankind well, yet wilt not choose me,
And Satan hates me, yet is loath to lose me.

2

Oh, my black soul! Now thou art summonèd
By sickness, death's herald and champion.
Thou art like a pilgrim which abroad hath done
Treason, and durst not turn to whence he is fled;
Or like a thief which, till death's doom be read,
Wisheth himself delivered from prison;
But damned and haled to execution,
Wisheth that still he might be imprisonèd.
Yet grace if thou repent thou canst not lack;
But who shall give thee that grace to begin?
O make thyself with holy mourning black,
And red with blushing, as thou art with sin;
Or wash thee in Christ's blood, which hath this might,
That being red, it dyes red souls to white.

3

This is my play's last scene; here heavens appoint
My pilgrimage's last mile; and my race
Idly yet quickly run, hath this last pace,
My span's last inch, my minutes' latest point;
And gluttonous death will instantly unjoint
My body and soul, and I shall sleep a space;
Or presently, I know not, see that face
Whose fear already shakes my every joint.
Then, as my soul to heaven her first seat takes flight,
And earth-born body in the earth shall dwell,
So fall my sins, that all may have their right
To where they're bred, and would press me, to hell.
Impute me righteous, thus purged of evil,
For thus I leave the world, the flesh, and devil.

4

At the round earth's imagined corners blow
Your trumpets, angels, and arise, arise
From death, you numberless infinities
Of souls, and to your scattered bodies go;
All whom the flood did, and fire shall o'erthrow,
All whom war, dearth, age, agues, tyrannies,
Despair, law, chance, hath slain, and you whose eyes
Shall behold God, and never taste death's woe.
But let them sleep, Lord, and me mourn a space;
For if above all these my sins abound,
'Tis late to ask abundance of thy grace
When we are there: here on this holy ground
Teach me how to repent; for that's as good
As if thou'dst sealed my pardon with thy blood.

5

If poisonous minerals, and if that tree
Whose fruit threw death on else immortal us,
If lecherous goats, if serpents envious
Cannot be damned, alas, why should I be?
Why should intent or reason born in me
Make sins, else equal, in me more heinous?
And, mercy being easy and glorious
To God, in his stern wrath why threatens he?
But who am I that dare dispute with thee?
O God, oh, of thine only worthy blood,
And my tears, make a heavenly Lethean flood,
And drown in it my sins' black memory.
That thou remember them, some claim as debt;
I think it mercy, if thou wilt forget.

6

Death be not proud, though some have callèd thee
Mighty and dreadful, for thou art not so;
For those whom thou think'st thou dost overthrow
Die not, poor death, nor yet canst thou kill me.
From rest and sleep, which but thy pictures be,
Much pleasure, then from thee much more must flow;
And soonest our best men with thee do go,
Rest of their bones, and souls' delivery.
Thou art slave to fate, chance, kings, and desperate men,
And dost with poison, war, and sickness dwell;
And poppy or charms can make us sleep as well
And better than thy stroke; why swell'st thou then?
One short sleep past, we wake eternally,
And death shall be no more; death, thou shalt die.

7

Spit in my face, ye Jews, and pierce my side;
Buffet and scoff, scourge and crucify me;
For I have sinned, and sinned, and only he
Who could do no iniquity hath died.
But by my death cannot be satisfied
My sins, which pass the Jews' impiety:
They killed once an inglorious man, but I
Crucify him daily, being now glorified.
Oh, let me then his strange love still admire;
Kings pardon, but he bore our punishment.
And Jacob came clothed in vile harsh attire
But to supplant, and with gainful intent:
God clothed himself in vile man's flesh, that so
He might be weak enough to suffer woe.

8

Why are we by all creatures waited on?
Why do the prodigal elements supply
Life and food to me, being more pure than I,
Simple, and further from corruption?
Why brook'st thou, ignorant horse, subjection?
Why dost thou, bull and boar, so seelily
Dissemble weakness, and by one man's stroke die,
Whose whole kind you might swallow and feed upon?
Weaker I am, woe is me, and worse than you;
You have not sinned, nor need be timorous.
But wonder at a greater wonder; for to us
Created nature doth these things subdue,
But their Creator, whom sin nor nature tied,
For us, his creatures and his foes, hath died.

9

What if this present were the world's last night?
Mark in my heart, O soul, where thou dost dwell,
The picture of Christ crucified, and tell
Whether that countenance can thee affright.
Tears in his eyes quench the amazing light;
Blood fills his frowns, which from his pierced head fell;
And can that tongue adjudge thee unto hell,
Which prayed forgiveness for his foes' fierce spite?
No, no; but as in my idolatry
I said to all my profane mistresses,
Beauty of pity, foulness only is
A sign of rigour: so I say to thee,
To wicked spirits are horrid shapes assigned;
This beauteous form assures a piteous mind.

10

Batter my heart, three-personed God; for you
As yet but knock, breathe, shine, and seek to mend;
That I may rise and stand, o'erthrow me and bend
Your force to break, blow, burn, and make me new.
I, like an usurped town to another due,
Labour to admit you, but oh, to no end;
Reason, your viceroy in me, me should defend,
But is captived, and proves weak or untrue.
Yet dearly I love you, and would be lovèd fain,
But am betrothed unto your enemy:
Divorce me, untie or break that knot again,
Take me to you, imprison me; for I
Except you enthral me never shall be free,
Nor ever chaste, except you ravish me.

11

Thou hast made me; and shall thy work decay?
Repair me now, for now mine end doth haste;
I run to death, and death meets me as fast,
And all my pleasures are like yesterday.
I dare not move my dim eyes any way;
Despair behind, and death before, doth cast
Such terror, and my feeble flesh doth waste
By sin in it, which it towards hell doth weigh.
Only thou art above, and when towards thee
By thy leave I can look, I rise again;
But our old subtle foe so tempteth me
That not one hour myself I can sustain.
Thy grace may wing me to prevent his art,
And thou like adamant draw mine iron heart.

12

I am a little world made cunningly
Of elements, and an angelic sprite;
But black sin hath betrayed to endless night
My world's both parts, and oh, both parts must die.
You which beyond that heaven which was most high
Have found new spheres, and of new lands can write,
Pour new seas in mine eyes, that so I might
Drown my world with my weeping earnestly,
Or wash it, if it must be drowned no more:
But oh, it must be burnt! Alas, the fire
Of lust and envy hath burnt it heretofore,
And made it fouler. Let their flames retire,
And burn me, O Lord, with a fiery zeal
Of thee and thy house, which doth in eating heal.

13

Since she whom I loved hath paid her last debt
To nature, and to hers and my good is dead,
And her soul early into heaven ravishèd,
Wholly on heavenly things my mind is set.
Here the admiring her my mind did whet
To seek thee, God; so streams do show the head:
But though I have found thee, and thou my thirst hast fed,
A holy thirsty dropsy melts me yet.
But why should I beg more love, whenas thou
Dost woo my soul, for hers offering all thine?
And dost not only fear lest I allow
My love to saints and angels, things divine,
But in thy tender jealousy dost doubt
Lest the world, flesh, yea, devil, put thee out?

14

Show me, dear Christ, thy spouse so bright and clear.
What, is it she which on the other shore
Goes richly painted? Or which, robbed and tore,
Laments and mourns in Germany and here?
Sleeps she a thousand, then peeps up one year?
Is she self truth, and errs? Now new, now outwore?
Doth she, and did she, and shall she evermore
On one, on seven, or on no hill appear?
Dwells she with us, or, like adventuring knights,
First travel we to seek, and then make love?
Betray, kind husband, thy spouse to our sights,
And let mine amorous soul court thy mild dove;
Who is most true and pleasing to thee then
When she's embraced and open to most men.

15

Oh, to vex me contraries meet in one:
Inconstancy unnaturally hath begot
A constant habit, that when I would not,
I change in vows, and in devotion.
As humorous is my contrition
As my profane love, and as soon forgot;
As riddlingly distempered, cold and hot,
As praying, as mute; as infinite, as none.
I durst not view heaven yesterday; and today
In prayers and flattering speeches I court God;
Tomorrow I quake with true fear of his rod.
So my devout fits come and go away
Like a fantastic ague: save that here
Those are my best days when I shake with fear.

NOTES

SIR THOMAS WYATT

Wyatt's sonnets, which survive in various manuscripts, were first printed in Tottel's *Songs and Sonets* (1557), republished frequently through the sixteenth century. This selection is based on Muir's edition of his collected poems (1949).

1 (Muir 7). A reconstruction of Petrarch's *Una candida cerva nell'erbe m'apparve* ('A fair hind appeared to me in the meadow'). The hind symbolized Laura; the poet pursued her while she eluded him, until he recognized that she belonged only to God. Wyatt turns the visionary experience into a hunt after a wayward mistress desired by many. See discussions of the sonnet by Bateson (141–2), Lever (26–7), and Thomson (1) (225), (2) (39).

4. Wyatt is but one of many pursuers. *6. Deer.* Capitalized in mss. to bring out the symbolism and the wordplay on 'dear'. *13. 'Noli...am'.* 'Touch me not, for I belong to Caesar'. The Latin is from Christ's words in the Vulgate version of John xx. 17; 'Caesar' in this context could mean God. The line comes from sixteenth century commentaries on Petrarch's sonnet, but in Wyatt's rendering this becomes ambiguous; 'Caesar' could mean the king, with the 'deer' as a court lady. Wyatt had been intimate with Anne Boleyn before her marriage.

2 (Muir 28). Based on Petrarch's *Pasa la nave mia colma d'obblio* ('My ship passes on, laden with oblivion'), a conceit widely imitated (cf. *Amor.* 14, *ShS.* 39. 5–8, *Idea* 2). The lover is allegorized as a ship in storm, steered by Love; the wind is his sighs, the rain his tears, the cloud his lady's disdain, etc.

1. charged with forgetfulness. Weighted down with the lady's neglect. *4. my Lord.* Love. *5. in readiness.* Prepared for shipwreck. *8. trusty fearfulness.* A mixture of trust and fear (the oxymoron is typical of the contradictions of love stressed in the romance tradition). *10. weared.* Combines the senses of 'wearied' and 'worn'. *12. The...hid.* Literally by the storm, allegorically for the lover's inscrutable fate.

3 (Muir 92). Through the conventional call to lovers to celebrate May Day (cf. *Amor.* 26) Wyatt laments the mishaps of his career at court.

1. abundance. Pronounced in the French manner, with first and last syllables stressed. *2. lust.* Pleasure. *joyful jollity.* Alliterative phrasing in the English medieval tradition. *4. observance.* Stressed like 'abundance', l.1. *6. haps most unhappy.* Mischanced chances. *9. Sephame.* An astrologer of the time. *9–10. my nativity...May.* The horoscope showed he would be unlucky under the planet in the ascendant in the zodiacal sign of May. *12–13.* Wyatt was imprisoned in May 1534 for riotous behaviour, and in May 1536 on charges of adultery with Queen Anne Boleyn. He was released, but Anne was executed; Wyatt witnessed the beheading of her five alleged lovers on Tower Hill. A Blage ms.

poem probably by Wyatt has the line 'These bloody days have broken my heart'.

4 (Muir 139). The truculence of this address to a fickle mistress is underscored by the use of 'not' as a recurrent ending.

2. such cause. Cause for railing and jesting. *5-6.* 'If you were true to me, I should hate to see you behaving with such unkindness towards others'. *7. so.* So fickle. *be kind.* 'Do me this favour'. *8.* 'Even if it does annoy me, still do not (rail or jest)'.

5 (Muir 145). Formally one of Wyatt's most accomplished sonnets, 'of entirely English stamp with its pure monosyllabic diction, its masculine rhymes, its unobtrusive use of alliteration for knitting together the verse texture' (Lever 30).

1. Divers doth use. 'Various persons are accustomed'. *8. otherwhere doth grow* Adhere elsewhere. *12. feed.* i.e. with promises. *13. of kind.* In the way of nature.

6 (Muir 173). Adapted from Petrarch's *Rotta è l'alta colonna e 'l verde lauro* ('The high column is fallen, and the green laurel'), lamenting the deaths of his friend Colonna and his beloved Laura. Wyatt alludes instead to the fall of Thomas Cromwell, his patron and protector, after the death of Jane Seymour.

1. pillar. From Petrarch's *colonna*, without the Italian wordplay. The second Italian pun, *lauro-Laura*, is omitted. *2. stay.* Support. *5. unhap...hap.* Misfortune ...chance. *6. bark and rind.* i.e. external appearance and inner truth. *8. do it relent.* Abates the mourning. *10. What...more.* 'What more is possible for me...?' *11.* On the alliteration here and in l.14, cf. **3**.2 and note.

HENRY HOWARD, EARL OF SURREY

Surrey's sonnets were first published with Wyatt's in Tottel's *Songs and Sonets* (1557). The text here is based on the edition of his poems by Emrys Jones (1966).

1 (Jones 4). Based on Petrarch's *Amor, che nel pensier mio* ('Love, which in my thoughts'). Love, as in the romance tradition, is a lord, whose castle is built in the poet's heart. The rhyme units make three quatrains and a couplet, while the syntax of ll.12-14 forms tercet units, following Italian sestet structure.

1, 3, 4. The strong opening stresses capture the forcefulness of Petrarch's sonnet. *2. seat.* Habitation. *6. doubtful hope.* The oxymoron expresses the 'contraries' of love. *7. shadow.* Conceal. *8. She* (l.5) is the subject, *Her smiling grace* the object, of *converteth. 9-10.* Petrarch has *Che poss' io far, temendo il mio signore* ('What can I do, when my own lord is afraid?'). *13.* Adapted from Surrey's translation of Virgil, *Aeneid* II: *mene efferre pedem, genitor* (Jones).

2 (Jones 29). One of three published sonnets on the death of Sir Thomas Wyatt, a close friend of Surrey's.

1. Divers...diversely. Various persons in various ways. *2-3.* Refers to Wyatt's enemies Suffolk, Bonner, Bishop of London, and Heynes, who were responsible for his impeachment and imprisonment in January 1541. *2. in...head.* Face to face with the living man. *3. Lurked.* Waited in ambush. *whose breasts.* Object of *sown. 4.* Caesar was reported to have wept when the head of his rival Pompey was brought to him; his tears became a byword for hypocrisy. *7. Whose...brake.* Whose designs were frustrated. *10. tempered.* Blended in proper proportions (as was said in Antony's last words on Brutus, *Julius Caesar* v). *13–14. avail As Pyramus.* 'Are as unavailing as those of Pyramus, (who)...' *14.* The love story of Pyramus and Thisbe, told in Ovid's *Metamorphoses* IV, was considered tragic till Shakespeare's parody in *Midsummer Night's Dream* made it seem ridiculous. The simile puts love for friendship and the fatal lion for the king.

3 (Jones 32). Ostensibly refers to Sardanapalus, whose sensuality and political ineptitude made him a type of the degenerate despot. Placed in a group of poems alluding to Surrey's friends and enemies, the sonnet is almost certainly a veiled execration of Henry VIII.

3–4. Sardanapalus was defeated by the king of the Medes through his profligacy and neglect of martial affairs. *5.* 'The blows of swords seemed strange after the impact of kisses'. *6. targe.* Target, shield. *8. above...charge.* Heavier than a garland worn at feasts. *11. unpatient of.* Unable to bear. *13 time of wealth.* In time of prosperity. *storms.* Adversity. *14.* The suicide was described in Lydgate's *Fall of Princes* as 'more bestial than like a manly man' (Jones).

4 (Jones 35). An epitaph for Thomas Clere, Surrey's companion and squire-at-arms, who died of wounds received at the siege of Montreuil in September 1544 while defending his master.

1. Clere was born at Ormesby, Norfolk, and buried in the chapel of the Howards in Lambeth. Surrey adapts Virgil's supposed epitaph for himself: *Mantua me genuit...tenet nunc Parthenope* ('Mantua gave me birth, Parthenope now holds me'). *2. of the...hight.* 'Though called one of the house of Cleremont'. Clere was associated with the Howards by blood, marriage, and knightly prowess. *3.* The Ormondes, Clere's ancestors, were linked with the Howards by his uncle's marriage. *4. thy cousin.* Anne Boleyn. *5. Shelton.* Mary Shelton, Clere's mistress, was Anne Boleyn's cousin. *chase.* Archaic form of 'chose'. *7. Kelsall.* A Scottish town burned by English troops in 1542. *8. Landrecy.* (Ms. 'Laundersey'). Besieged in 1543 by forces commanded by Sir John Wallop, under whom Surrey and Clere served. *Boulogne.* (Ms. 'Bullen'). Surrendered in 1544. *9. Montreuil.* (Ms. 'Muttrell'). Where Clere received his fatal wound. *hopeless...recure.* Without any hope of recovery. *11. pining death.* Death came seven months after the wound. *13. if love...cost.* 'If love, care, or money could have availed'. *14. timely.* Early.

SIR PHILIP SIDNEY

Astrophel and Stella

(See Introd., pp. 8–11.) Sidney's brilliant career as courtier, diplomat, scholar and poet, was cut short by his death after the battle of Zutphen in 1586, when he was thirty-two. Many of his sonnets are interspersed in the prose romance *Arcadia* (c. 1580, publ. 1590); his finest verse, however, is in the sequence *Astrophel and Stella*. First printed in a pirated version in 1591, and in an edition authorized by his sister in 1598, its influence was profound throughout the Elizabethan age. The most comprehensive modern edition is by Ringler (1962).

Title. *Astrophel*. Ringler's edition prints *Astrophil*. Both the 1591 Quarto and 1598 Folio, authorized by Sidney's sister the Countess of Pembroke, have 'Astrophel'. The name appears three times in the complete text, in Song viii. 5, 73 and ix. 27, where it is always 'Astrophel' except in two incomplete manuscripts. These are BM. Add. Ms. 15232, with 'Astrophil' at viii. 5 but 'Astrophel' at viii. 73, and ix omitted; and a Cambridge Ms., described by Ringler as 'exceptionally inaccurate', with 'Astrophil' at ix. 27. The Countess of Pembroke knew her brother's handwriting, where 'e' and 'i' are clearly distinguishable, and would hardly have let his famous sonnet sequence be printed with a flagrant mistake in the title. 'Astrophel' is the spelling of Daniel, Spenser, Nashe and others, and has been followed down the centuries. While 'Astrophil' (lover of a star) is good Greek, this is not an adequate reason for changing the familiar title, especially when the textual supports are so slender.

1 (i). 'The sonnet does not disclaim artifice and convention but proceeds towards an ironic reminder of the energy that lies behind artifice' (Kalstone, 129).

1–4. Based on *gradatio*, the rhetorical 'ladder' leading from premise to premise, *2. she, dear she.* From the 1598 Folio, and providing a suitable balance of stresses. Ringler instead chooses a damaged line in the British Museum Ms. 'thee (deer...he)', and reconstructs it as 'the deare She'. *8. sunburned brain.* (Owing to working too long in the light of others' work.) *11. feet.* (1) Guiding steps; (2) Units of verse. *13–14.* See Introd., p. 9.

2 (ii).

1. a dribbed shot. 'An arrow falling feebly and thus unable to pierce a corselet' (*Shakespeare's England* ii. 381). *3. in mine of time.* (Substitutes modern siege tactics (undermining) for the conventional arrows of love.) *8. partial lot.* Biased decision. *9. footstep.* Token of freewill implied in agreement (l. 7). *10–11.* The simile was based on reports of contemporary travellers in Muscovy, contemporary name for Russia. These were incorporated later in Hakluyt's *Navigations* (1589, 1598). *14. feeling.* Heart-felt.

3 (iii). Ironical praise of literary affections in ll. 1–8 is undercut by the colloquial directness of the sestet.

1. Sisters Nine. Muses of Greek mythology. *3. Pindar's apes.* Imitators of the Greek Odes of Pindar (c. 500 B.C.), whose resplendent style was often copied by Renaissance poets. Ronsard wrote: '*Le premier de France / J'ai pindarisé.*' *4. pied flowers.* Parti-coloured ornaments of speech; *pied* may hint at a fool's motley. *6. new-found tropes.* Many works appeared listing rhetorical devices under new, sometimes far-fetched names, notably Puttenham's *Art of English Poesy* (1589). *problems.* Topics. *8.* Indicating the laboured similes of Lyly's *Euphues* (1578). *9. no...one.* i.e. Stella.

4 (v).

1–4. Stating the sixteenth-century commonplace of a 'correspondence' between the monarch ruling the body politic and reason governing the human body.

2. heavenly part. Reason, of divine origin. *10–11. shade...mixed.* In Platonist teaching the soul coming to earth must mix with the four elements in matter, which resist or may deform the spirit. Physical beauty was a shadow (*shade*) of ideal beauty. *12–13.* Cf. Hebrews xi. 13–16: 'pilgrims on the earth...they desire a better country, that is, an heavenly'. A proverbial image.

5 (VIII). Conceits of Cupid taking refuge with the poet and setting his heart on fire went back to classical erotic verse. Sidney provides a contemporary setting. See John, 67; Lever, 66–9.

1–4. Love here is a fugitive after the Turkish conquest of Greece. If Cyprus —the home of Venus—is meant by 'Greece', this may allude to its fall in 1573. *5. these north climes.* The English climate is associated with Stella's 'coldness'. *9. beamy.* Emitting beams of light (currently believed to be the means of sight). *14.* (Instead of being conventionally capricious or vindictive, Love is associated with the poet as a victim of circumstance.)

6 (X).
3. the Muses' hill. Mount Parnassus, home of the Muses in Greek mythology. *4.* Alludes to the golden apples of the Hesperides, located by tradition in the west. *5.* 'Or turn to astronomy or theology'. *8. powers of thoughts.* Faculties of the mind, as opposed to *will* (sensual desire). *11. downright.* (1) Frank, as against *cunning*; (2) vertically downwards.

7 (XV).
1–6. Cf. Sidney, *Defence of Poetry*: 'that honey-flowing Matron Eloquence, apparelled...with coursing of a letter, as if...bound to follow the method of a dictionary: another time with figures and flowers, extremely winter-starved'. *2. Parnassus.* (Cf. **6**.3). *6.* A parody of alliterative technique. *8. denizened.* Naturalized, but of alien origin. *10. inward touch.* Innate aptitude.

8 (XVII). Based, like **5**, on a classical conceit revived by Renaissance poets. Pontano's version was subtitled *De Stella*. On Sidney's rendering see Lever, 62–6.

1. Cupid is the subject, *His mother dear* the object. *2. Mars.* God of war, lover of Venus. *her love.* Love of her. *9. it.* The child. *11. arrows infinite.* An infinite number of arrows. *14. shrewd turns.* Naughty tricks.

9 (XVIII).
1. shent. Financially ruined (still a northern idiom). *2.* Cf. Matt. xii. 36: 'they shall give account thereof in the day of judgement'. *3–6.* Underlying the image is the gospel parable of the talents, together with the Senecan view of life as a debt owed to nature. *4. have.* Plural form with singular subject (a common Elizabethan usage), probably influenced by *goods*. *9. toys.* Trifles.

10 (XX). See Kalstone, 148–50.
1–4. Cupid aiming his dart becomes a highwayman or sniper with a musket, lurking behind a bush. *7. that sweet black.* Stella's eyelashes. *9. thereby.* By the way. *13. dart.* The conventional arrow now replaces the 'bullet' of l.4.

11 (XXI).
1. my friend. Possibly Edward Dyer. *6. gyres.* Gyrations (Ringler, from *giers*). The 1598 Folio has *yeeres* ('years'), perhaps a scribal substitution or misreading for the stronger, less familiar term. (See note to **26**.8.) *6–7. Nobler desires.* Either nobler impulses, or towards someone of nobler rank. The ambiguity is tactful. *9. mad March.* His boyhood.

12 (XXIV). A sonnet of execration against Lord Rich, who married Penelope Devereux in November 1581.
2. hatching. Closing up, hoarding. *3. Tantal's smart.* In Homer, Tantalus was punished by having to stand in water he was unable to drink, with fruit over-

head which he was unable to grasp. Renaissance commentators presented him as an emblem of avarice. *4. more blissed, more wretched.* The luckier they are, the more unhappy. *11.* According to Sir Charles Blount, who later became Penelope's lover, 'Instead of a Comforter he [Rich] did study in all ways to torment her'.

13 (xxviii).

1. Perhaps alluding to Spenser's *Faerie Queene*, or to Bruno's allegorical *Eroici Furori*, dedicated to Sidney. *2.* Transforming other writers' characters into symbolic figures (e.g. Spenser's conversion of Ariosto's Bradamante, in *Orlando Furioso*, to Britomart). *4. brazen fame.* Immortal repute; cf. *Love's Labour's Lost* 1.i. 1-2: 'Let fame...Live registered upon our brazen tombs'. *8. nations.* Universal social custom. *12-13.* The flames do not serve, as in alchemy, to refine some 'quintessence', but are simply exhaled in words.

14 (xxx).

1. the Turkish new moon. The Islamic emblem. Between March and June 1582 newsletters predicted a Turkish attack upon Spanish possessions (John). *3. Poles' right king.* Stefan Batóry, crowned in 1576. He invaded Russia in 1580, and besieged Pskov until the end of 1581. *leave of host.* With wordplay on *host*. Either the support of an adequate army, or permission of the Russians. *4. ill-made fire.* The Poles used red-hot cannon balls in siege operations. *5.* Recalling Caesar's hackneyed statement that all Gaul was divided into three parts; applied to the contemporary factions of Catholics, Huguenots and 'Politiques'. *6. the Dutch...diets.* Refers to the Germans (commonly called 'Dutch') and the Diet (assembly) of Augsburg, July–September 1582. *7. now...lost.* Breda and Tournay fell to the Spaniards in 1581, other towns of importance in 1582. *8. Orange tree.* William of Orange, who ruled the Dutch 1576–84. *9-10.* Sir Henry Sidney was Lord Deputy of Ireland until early 1582; the *golden bit* was the 'cess', a levy on land-owners to provision English troops stationed in Ulster. *11.* A period of turbulence (*weltering*) in Scotland ended in August 1582. The 1598 Folio has 'If in the Scotch Court be no weltring yet', perhaps due to later revision.

15 (xxxi). See Kalstone, 162–5, also Muir (2), 29.

1-4. The subtle interposing of long syllables and variations of stress give this quatrain its quality of rapt wonder. *4. That busy archer.* Love. *9. even of fellowship.* The fancy of having a fellow-sufferer in love is paralleled in **5**. *14.* Probably a transposition: 'Do they call ungratefulness up there a virtue?' But Muir (2) accepts the regular prose order: 'the last [question] is aimed at himself for stigmatizing Stella's virtue, or chastity, as ingratitude'.

16 (xxxiii).

5. rent. A variant of 'rend'. *6-8.* Astrophel admits that he had no prior claim on Stella, either marital or moral. *9-11.* In 1576, when Penelope Devereux was 13, her dying father expressed the wish that Philip Sidney, then 21, should match with her. When Sidney met her in 1581 she was already about to marry Rich. *12. by rising morn.* Probably alluding to the lost opportunity of 1576.

17 (xxxiv). A sonnet about whether to write a sonnet, in the form of internal dialogue perhaps suggested by Senecan drama (cf. *Richard III*, v.iii.182–92). *3. glasses.* Mirrors serving to reflect. *7. fond ware.* Articles valued by fools.

18 (XXXIX). See Lever, 88.

2. bating-place. Place of refreshment on a journey. From the 1598 'baiting place'. But 'bathing place' in the 1591 edn. makes good sense in apposition to *balm*, and inspired Shakespeare's invocation: 'the innocent sleep...sore labour's bath, Balm of hurt minds' (*Macbeth* II.ii.36-9). *5. proof.* Tried strength. *prease.* Press, throng. *11. rosy.* Pertaining to secrecy or silence, as in '*sub rosa*' (Ringler).

19 (XL).

1. The line, a unit to itself, sets the poem in the framework of a soliloquy, charged with religious attitudes subserving a romance situation. (See Greville and Donne for the converse approach.) *3-4.* Sidney's own self-esteem and sense of vocation are involved, not merely the woes of a fictitious Astrophel. *5-6.* (Stella, as a 'star', may shed her 'influence' from *virtue's throne*.) *8-11.* The romance image of the heart as a captured fortress is applied in a personal context; this gathers to itself biblical associations in ll. 12-14. Cf. Donne, *HS* 10. *14.* The lover's heart as a temple to his mistress was a traditional sonnet image (cf. *Amor.* 10). But here the destruction of the Jerusalem Temple is evoked, through its Christian correlative the heart: Cf. 1 Cor. vi.19: 'know ye not that your heart is the temple of the holy ghost...?'

20 (XLVII).

2. black beams. The rays from Stella's eyes. *burning marks.* Brands of slavery. *4.* 'for whose neck such a yoke of tyranny is fitting'. Cf. **2.**10-11. *9-14.* The passive self-abasement of the octave is replaced by an energetic 'awakening', expressed in dramatic speech-rhythms.

21 (XLVIII). An acutely emotional recoil from the attitudes of **20**, but reflecting the same tensions.

14. From Petrarch's *Un modo di pietate, occider tosto.*

22 (LIII).

2. staves. Staffs; shafts of a spear or lance. *6. Mars's livery.* Armour. *7. I would no less.* Compare our 'that's all I need'. *9.* A beam of light reflected from a window pane is fancifully identified with the rays of Stella's eyes. *12. trumpet's.* Alternatively 'trumpet' (in the quartos). Ringler's 'trumpets'' seems an unnecessary change. *13. beat the air.* Probably 'beating' to provoke combat, as one beats up game.

23 (LXII).

3. unfelt. i.e. by Stella herself. *8.* Stella confirms Sidney's own doubts, expressed in **11** and **19**. *12-13.* Cf. **20.**8.

24 (LXIV).

1. these counsels. As in **23**. 6-11. *10. Caesar's bleeding fame.* Caesar's ambition, which led to his death.

25 (LXVI). Marks a new stage in the courtship; Stella gives him some encouragement.

3-4. quick apprehending...show. A seizing upon imaginary comforts. *6. Fortune's wheel's.* The wheel of fortune, carrying men up and down, was a favourite medieval symbol. 1598 Folio and most texts have *Fortunes wheeles*; Ringler emends to 'Fortune wheeles'. But apostrophes, often omitted in manuscripts, were surely implied here. *14. They.* Stella's eyes.

26 (LXVIII).

1–8. The impetuous speech-rhythms depart from staple iambics, giving life to the rhetorical tropes, the 'gradation' in ll.1–2 (cf. **1**.1–4), the appositions in ll. 4 and 8, and the mythological reference in l. 6. *6.* Amphion was the son of Zeus; his magic skill in playing on the lyre caused the walls of Thebes to rise of their own accord. *Wed.* Be joined to. *8. blinded.* Ringler, Mona Wilson and most editors adopt the 2nd Quarto *kindled*, which is consistent with *fire* in l. 7 but rather commonplace. 1598 Folio has *blinded*, a forceful transferred epithet governed by *thy sight.* The less obvious word is more in keeping with the sonnet's emotional tension. *14. enjoy.* Playing on the word's sexual connotation.

27 (LXIX).

3. Envy, put out thine eyes. A common emblem, as in Spenser, *The Faerie Queene* I.iv. 31 : 'All in a kirtle of discoloured say He clothed was, ypainted full of eyes'. *5.* Cf. **11**.1. *12–14.* 'Stella's stipulation…occurs almost as an afterthought, and the implication…is that covenants must be made—and broken—by the experienced *politique*' (Kalstone, 172).

28 (LXXI). Remodelled, with striking divergences of outlook, from Petrarch's *Chi vuol veder.* See Lever, 58–62, Kalstone, 117–22. Instead of sun-like illumination, the lady's attributes are reason and virtue.

4. those fair lines. (1) Rows of words; (2) lineaments, features. (Petrarch's Laura was a revelation of nature and heaven; Stella, an edifying 'book'.) *7. night-birds.* 'the owl…is used variously to pictorialize avarice, envy, sloth and gluttony' (Ringler). *9–13.* The stress on Stella's virtuous influence replaces Petrarch's anticipations of Laura's death, and heightens the antithesis of the last line.

29 (LXXIV). Between this and **28** the 'Second Song' described the stealing of a kiss from Stella while she lay asleep and ended with the poet's self-reproach, 'Fool, more fool, for no more taking'.

1. Aganippe well. A spring at the foot of Mount Helicon, sacred to the Muses: drinking its water gave poetic inspiration. *2. Tempe.* The valley below Mount Olympus, home of the gods. *7. blackest…hell.* The river Styx, which flowed into a ravine, and thence reputedly to Hades. The most solemn oaths were sworn by it. *9–14.* The easy, idiomatic words and rhythms balance the learned allusiveness of the octave.

30 (LXXVI). As in **1**, the slow march of alexandrines leads to the startling conceit of the conclusion.

1. shining twins. Eyes. *5. Aurora.* The dawn. *13. stayed feet…walking head.* Feet unable to move, head in a state of dizziness. Ringler's 'staid' obscures the self-mockery of the transposed adjectives, leading to the climactic last line.

31 (LXXVIII).

5. others' harm, self-misery. Cause of harm to others, of misery to himself. *8.* He only cherishes (clings to) his 'joy' in order to injure it. *11. on thorns.* In painful anxiety: a common idiom. *14. horns.* (With play on cuckoldry).

32 (LXXXI). Cf. Spenser, *Amor.* 23.

*2. Or…or…*Whether they be…or… *5.* A Neoplatonic attitude, whose sincerity is undercut in the sestet. *8. shade out.* Sketch. *14. still still.* (1) Constantly; (2) secretly.

33 (LXXXIII). Suggested by Skelton's *Philip Sparrow*, addressed to his mistress's pet sparrow.

1. brother Philip. Skelton's name for the sparrow is Sidney's own. *3. your cut to keep.* To keep your distance, show respect. *14. Phip.* Common abbreviation of Philip.

34 (LXXXIV). On the occasion of a journey to a secret assignation with Stella.
1-4. Sidney's 'Muse' has her dwelling on the highway; i.e., he writes better on a journey than indoors. *1. Parnassus:* see note to **6**.3. *6. safeliest.* The modernised form of the 1598 'saflest', (1591 Quarto 'safliest'), stressing the secrecy of the encounter. *10. encroachment.* By private landowners; an abuse of the time.

35 (LXXXV). As in **30**. 13-14, he fears that his excitement will impede his functioning as a lover.
1. the house. (Where Astrophel and Stella will meet.) *3-4.* Lest the 'animal spirits' of sensation and motion, expanded by excessive joy, should overstrain his heart. *6. undercharge.* Subordinate duty. *11. wit to wonder ties.* Combines understanding with admiration. *13. the globe of weal.* The world of happiness, i.e. Stella's body. *love's indentures.* The joining of lips; indentures being legal agreements in duplicate with edges indented, so that, put together, they formed a single document. *14. Thou.* The heart.

36 (LXXXVII). Between this sonnet and **35** appear the 'Fourth Song' with its refrain 'No no, no no, my dear, let be'; LXXXVI on 'this change of looks'; and five songs, including 'In a grove most rich of shade', where Stella, at the dictates of 'Tyrant Honour', renounces Astrophel.
8. saddest. From 1598 Folio, as opposed to *sweetest*, l. 7. Ringler gives no authority for his 'sadded'.

37 (XCI). An apology for being attracted to other women in Stella's absence.
2. misled. Led away. *8. seeing jets black.* Either 'pieces of jet that can see, black eyes' (Ringler), or 'upon my seeing black jets (eyes)'. *11. wood-globes.* 'on which are depicted the arrangement of the constellations...they lack the brilliance and magnitude of the real stars in the sky' (Ringler).

38 (XCII).
1. good sir. Some acquaintance, unlikely to have been the 'friend' of **11**. *Indian.* i.e. fabulously precious. *3. cutted Spartans.* Notorious among the ancient Greeks for their curt, 'laconic' speech. *5. total.* Absolute (allowing no elaboration). *6. Phoenix.* Unique; from the mythical bird, only one of which at any single time was to be found on earth. Often used as a symbol of perfection. *9-14.* Cf. Rosalind's questions about Orlando: 'What said he? How looked he? Wherein went he?' etc., *As You Like It* III.ii.205ff.

39 (CI).
3. conclusions tries. Performs experiments. *8. weep in thee.* Weep while still giving an appearance of joy. *9. Love moans thy pain.* In apposition to l. 12, 'Nature with care sweats'. 1598 Folio has 'moues', a common misprint for 'mones', i.e. moans. *11. prest.* Ready, prepared (French *prêt*). *14. heaven stuff.* Heavenly material, i.e. Stella's physical beauty.

40 (CIII). Suggested by Petrarch's *Erano i capei*, especially his word-play on

Laura and *l'aura* ('the breezes'). But the treatment is individual and not in-compatible with some actual experience.

3. livery. Distinctive mark (like the badge worn by a nobleman's retainers). *9. Aeol's youths.* Children of Aeolus, ruler of the winds. *11. puffing kiss.* The winds' kiss, that puffed out Stella's hair.

41 (CV). On a momentary glimpse of Stella in her coach.

2. in…time. On such a promising occasion. *3. Dead glass.* (Addressed to his own insufficiently quick eye.) *6. dazzling race.* Unsteady vision (believed to come from beams projected by the eye). *7–8.* Stella's face, as a *heaven*, was sought in the sky; hence Astrophel did not look out for what might be on the road. *10. nectar.* Divine drink. *11. the page.* Pages or link-boys carried torches ahead of travellers to light their way through the streets at night. *12. your strife.* The eyes' effort to see.

42 (CVII).

7. lieutenancy. Delegated authority. *8. this great cause.* The allusion is uncertain. Sidney's father proposed in April 1582 that his son should succeed him as Lord Deputy of Ireland; but this came to nothing. In November 1585 Sir Philip sailed for the Netherlands, where he fought as a cavalry officer and was killed at Zutphen eleven months later. *both use and art.* Practice and skill; a blend of military valour and political aptitude. *9. as a queen.* The image is hard to dissociate from some actual mission of Queen Elizabeth.

Other Sonnets

43–4 come from a collection of 32 miscellaneous poems printed as an appendix to the 'Old' *Arcadia*. Many readers have felt that they are 'the only possible dramatic resolution for *Astrophel and Stella*' (Kalstone, 178). For the opposite view, see Ringler, 423–4. In any case, they have an intensity unmatched in Sidney's earlier poetry.

43

1. mark. Target. *2.* What floats on the surface of fancy, and underlies random speculation. *3. band.* Troop, company. *4.* Will (sexual appetite) imagined as a fabric on the loom, never completely woven; the metaphor may be a recollection of Penelope's weaving in the *Odyssey*, which kept her suitors in a state of permanent expectation. *7. brought.* Caused to become (OED). *13. hire.* Reward.

44. Written in the 'Surrey' verse form, like several sonnets of this collection, and unlike those of *Astrophel and Stella*.

3. that…rust. 'lay up for yourselves treasures in heaven, where neither moth nor rust can corrupt' (Matt. vi.20). *8.* (God's glory is revealed in nature, and man is given the faculty to perceive it.) *11. evil.* A monosyllable, identified with 'ill'. *Splendidis longum valedico nugis.* 'I bid a long farewell to glittering trifles.'

EDMUND SPENSER

Amoretti appeared, together with Spenser's marriage ode *Epithalamion*, in an apparently unauthorised edition in 1595. Though some earlier sonnets seem tenuously related to the sequence, the composition as a whole stands out as a highly distinctive treatment of courtship and betrothal. Written near the completion of Books IV–VI of *The Faerie Queene* (published 1596), the sonnets are imbued with Spenser's characteristic blend of Platonist philosophy, Christian faith, and Renaissance sensuousness.

1 (I). A skilful use of the 'Surrey' sonnet form combined with Spenser's interlacing rhymes. Eulogy mounts from 'lily hands' to 'lamping eyes', 'angel's look', and 'heaven's bliss'.
1. leaves. Sheets of paper. *2. dead-doing.* With power to inflict death. *6. lamping.* Shining like lamps: hence resembling the stars created 'for lights in the firmament' (Gen. i.15). *8. book.* As a repository for thoughts ('book and volume of my brain', *Hamlet* I.v. 103). *9–10. sacred…Helicon.* Cf. *AS* 29.1 and note. *10. whence…is.* Since Helicon was sacred to the Muses, this identifies the lady herself with a Muse. *12. soul's long-lacked food.* Cf. Romei, *The Courtier's Academy* (tr. Kepers 1598): 'the eyes…swallow down the idea of the beauty beloved, and transport it to the lover's heart'.

2 (II).
1. Unquiet. Restless. *bred.* Fostered (in the womb). *4. womb.* Figurative for heart, where the thought was bred (l. 1). *6. viper's brood.* Suggesting new-born energy. *8. food.* Cf. **1**.12.

3 (III).
1. sovereign. Supreme. *admire.* Marvel at. *2. witness the world.* Let the world bear witness. *3–4.* The lady is seen in Renaissance Platonic terms as an embodiment of spiritual love. Cf. Castiglione, *The Courtier* (tr. Hoby): 'the soul kindled in the most holy fire of true heavenly love…enjoyeth the sovereign happiness that cannot be comprehended of the senses', *5–8.* Ideal beauty, according to Castiglione, 'lightneth the subject where it shineth…like the sunbeams that strike against…fine gold'. *10. astonishment.* Loss of courage. *11. titles.* Claims to praise.

4 (IV). The sequence begins with the new year; spring is announced in **9**.
1. Janus' gate. The name of this Roman god was associated with *janua*, 'gate', and his chief festival was New Year's Day. Depicted with two faces, Janus looked before and back, and was invoked at the commencement of a new enterprise. Despite the association with January, the mention of 'spring…in his timely hour' may imply that 'new year' followed the traditional calendar, commencing on Lady Day, 25 March. *3. his passed date.* The occasion of new year's passing. *6. Love.* Personified as Eros, with wings and arrows (l. 8). *8. wanton.* Sportive.

5 (V).
1. heart's desire. Person desired by his heart. *2. portly.* Stately. *4. the world unworthy.* Resembles Petrarch's '*mondo cieco che vertù non cura*' ('blind world which cares not for virtue'). *9. praise…honour.* To be praised…to be honoured. *10. boldened.* Given courage. *14. self-pleasing.* Self-assured, pursuing its own course.

6 (VIII). Written in the Surrey form with separate rhyme units for each quatrain. This is perhaps Spenser's clearest statement of the lady's significance and the most lucid passage of self-examination in the sonnets.

1. the living fire. The pure fire of the empyrean, the highest sphere in the Ptolemaic universe, inhabited by God and his angels. *3. no eyes but joys.* The word-play is brought out in the old spelling 'ioyes'. *5. blinded guest.* Blindfold Cupid, traditionally shooting from the lady's eyes. *8. on...bound.* Directing their course towards heavenly beauty. (The Platonic 'ladder of ascent' led from earthly to spiritual beauties.)

7 (XIII).

1. port. Carriage, deportment. *3. embaseth.* Lowers. *4. temperature.* Balance of humours. (Cf. Surrey 2.10 and note.) *5.* The run-over of the quatrain into this fifth line adds weight to the apposition of *humblesse* and *majesty. 11. forlorn.* Spiritually lost. *12. hinders.* Combines the old sense 'harms' with the modern 'impedes'. *13.* 'Yet still deign to look on me, lowly as I am'.

8 (XV). Imitated from Desportes, *Diane* 1.32, '*Marchans, qui traversez*', but the couplet is Spenser's addition.

1. tradeful. Busily trading. *3. both the Indias.* East and West Indies. *4. needeth you.* Gives you need. *7. plain.* Perfect, clear. *10. her...ween.* 'Consider her forehead to be ivory'.

9 (XIX). Marks the advent of full spring, and celebrates the traditional May festivities of lovers, in which the lady takes no part.

1–4. The cuckoo is humanised as a trumpeter proclaiming the arrival of the May King, who is saluted by 'the choir of birds' (l. 5). *5. noise.* Music. *7.* Used, with minor variations, as the refrain of *Epithalamion. 10. that...ought.* Who should most honour it (Love). *11. his precept.* The command of King Love (to join in the May celebrations). *14. ere cuckoo end.* Before the cuckoo ceases his song (in June). *a rebel be.* Be considered a rebel against Love.

10 (XXII). Suggested by Desportes, *Diane* 1.43, '*Solitaire et pensif*', but modified to give the 'temple' a Christian quality unlike Desportes' pagan evocations. See Lever, 105–7. The 'holy season' is Lent.

1–4. Desportes said he would build, in some wood remote from the crowd, a temple to his 'chaste goddess'. Spenser means to show his devotion as other men do, finding some fit service for his 'sweet saint'. *5. within my mind.* The service of love will not be just an imitation of pagan rites. *9–12.* From Desportes: '*Mon oeil sera la lampe et la flamme immortelle, Qui me va consumant...Mon corps sera l'autel*'. It need not be supposed that Spenser implies a reference here to Ash Wednesday. *9. author.* Originator. *13. goddess.* A term out of place in this Christianised setting; but the association with 'saint', l. 4, is restored by 'thy dearest relics', l. 14.

11 (XXIII).

1–4. Alludes to Homer's episode in the *Odyssey* XIX. *2. web.* Woven fabric. *5. craft.* (1) Skill; (2) cunning. *conceive.* Devise. *6. importune suit.* Importunate pleading. *7–8.* (The conceit is strained, since here it is the poet who weaves, the lady who unweaves.) *9. when.* Whereas. *that.* That which. *12. my whole year's work.* A year of courtship is referred to much later, in **19**. This sonnet, like some others in *Amoretti*, may have originally belonged to another series.

12 (XXVII). Cf. **7**.

3. itself shall shroud. The dross (l. 2) will cover all such glory. *5. goodly idol.* Earthly beauty. *gay beseen.* Of good appearance. *6. doff.* Take off (clothing). *8.*

worship. Honour. *11. this verse, that never shall expire*. The promise to 'immortalise' the loved one's beauty in verse is a conventional flourish, rather than an essential theme, as in Shakespeare.

13 (XXXIII). Addressed to Spenser's friend Lodwick Bryskett, apologising for the delay in completing *The Faerie Queene*. (Books IV–VI were published in 1596.) The familiar tone is in marked contrast to the style of previous sonnets to the lady.

2. that most sacred Empress. Books I–III of *The Faerie Queene* (1590) were dedicated to Elizabeth I as 'most high, mighty, and magnificent Empress'. The Queen was *sacred* both as a monarch and as Head of the Church. *4.* 'That may enhance the praises she receives in life with more praise after death.' *5. of grace*. By way of pardon. *8. all were it*. Even though it were. *11. fit*. Anguish.

14 (XXXIV). An original treatment of Petrarch's much imitated metaphor depicting the lover as a storm-tossed ship. (Cf. Wyatt 2.)

2. by conduct of. Directed by. *5. star*. The lady. (Sidney's 'Stella' also meant 'star'.) *9–12*. The hopeful tone contrasts with the traditional imagery of cumulative despair. *10. Helice*. A star to the north: its name suggested wordplay on Eliza (or Elizabeth) Boyle, who married Spenser in 1595. *lodestar*. North or guiding star (cf. *ShS*. 39.7. 'the star to every wandering bark.)

15 (XL).
1. amiable. Loving. *3–4*. Cf. *Faerie Queene* VI.x.11: 'There did he see...An hundred naked maidens lily white, All ranged in a ring'. The 'maidens' symbolized the loving looks of Amoret, or true love, in contrast to the wounding darts of Eros in the romance tradition. *5–8*. (Contrast the imagery of storm and sunshine in *ShS* 15, 16). *9. sits on spray*. (Harks back to the alliterative phrases of the medieval English lyric.)

16 (LI). The monument image, derived, as in *ShS* 22, from Ovid and Horace, here signifies not poetic immortalization, but the 'hardness' of the lady's virtue.

5. lover's trade. The ways of lovers. *9. attend*. Wait patiently. *10. allure*. Attract. *14. greater*. Then a near-rhyme to 'get her', l. 13.

17 (LVIII). Entitled 'By [i.e. concerning] her that is most assured to herself'. This sonnet and **18** are in the form of question and answer.

3. that. The lady's self-assurance. *5–8*. Combines the biblical allusion in Matt. xxvi.41, 'the flesh is weak', with Ovid's *tempus edax* ('devouring time'), *Metamorphoses* xv. *7. preyed*. Preyed on, despoiled. *9. Ne none*. Nor is there any. *11–12*. Implying the medieval image of fortune's wheel.

18 (LIX).
1. Thrice happy. Cf. the triple 'happy' in **1**. *4*. 'Nor, frightened by a worse outcome, to move from her way at anything that might befall'. *5–8*. The ship-in-storm image of **14** is transferred from the poet to the lady. *7, 8. ne aught*. Nor to any degree. *9–10. Such...foes*. Perhaps anticipating the slanders complained of in **33**. *11. stay*. Support. *12*. A distortion of normal prose order: 'bends herself neither to one (*spite*) nor the other(*favour*)'.

19 (LX). Commemorating a year of courtship. Spenser is now over forty.
1. Refers to astrologers who study the concentric spheres in which, according to the Ptolemaic system, the sun, moon and planets revolved. *2. his sundry year*.

The time taken by each particular planet, reckoned in 'sun years', to return to its original place in the sphere. *4.* 'Mars, for example, has a planetary year of sixty sun years'. *5–6. since...move.* Since the poet came under Cupid's influence. *9–10.* The conceit of 'lovers' books' turns the subjective impression of a forty years' courtship into an imagined 'planetary year' of Cupid, forty years long according to the solar calendar. *13.* Let the lady, symbolised as a 'planet' called Cupid, move more swiftly in her affections. *14. or else short my days.* 'Or not let me live in suffering for so long'.

20 (LXI).

1. The Lady is seen as a Christian-Platonic manifestation of divine beauty. *2. saint...idol.* A typically Spenserian (and Renaissance) yoking of Christian and pagan epithets: compare 'saint...goddess' in **10**.4, 13. *3. dare not.* Do not dare (imperative, addressed to himself). *11. what...but.* 'What can one suppose but that...' *14. men of mean degree.* As compared with the status of angels and saints.

21 (LXII). Marks a second new year, which may, like the first (cf. **4**), commence in March.

2. compassed course. Regulated cycle. *6. minds.* Inclinations. *7. forepast.* Already passed. *11. blend.* Blemish.

22 (LXIII). A third variant on the ship-in-storm image of **14** and **18**: the end of the turbulent voyage is in sight.

3. dangerous dismay. Loss of courage in the presence of danger, with play on 'danger' in the romance sense of feminine hostility. *7. fraught with store.* Furnished with abundance. *8. alive.* In life. *14. eternal bliss.* The spiritual concept is fused with the idea of happiness in earthly love.

23 (LXIV). Cf. *AS* 32. Spenser's sonnet repeatedly echoes the Song of Solomon, believed to symbolize the marriage of Christ and the Church. Physical love is thus given a sacramental quality.

1. Coming...lips. The kiss was seen by Renaissance Platonists as 'a coupling of souls together'. The passage in Castiglione's *The Courtier* referring to this idea quoted the Song of Solomon as authority. *2. a garden of sweet flowers.* Cf. Song of Solomon iv.12: 'A garden enclosed is my sister, my spouse'. *5–12.* While the similes are English, the cadences are biblical: cf. Sol. v.10–13: 'My beloved is white and ruddy...His eyes are as the eyes of doves...His cheeks are as a bed of spices, as sweet flowers; his lips like lilies.' *5. gillyflowers.* Cloves. *7. belamours.* An unidentified, probably symbolical flower; the word means 'loved ones'. *12. jessamines.* Jasmine.

24 (LXVII). Follows Tasso's variant (*Questa fera gentil*) on the Petrarchan metaphor of the hind that escaped the hunter (cf. Wyatt 1).

7. the gentle deer. Tasso's *fera gentil* ('gentle wild one'). *deer* is spelt 'deare' in the early editions, substituting English wordplay for the Italian oxymoron. *9–12.* Spenser humanises the deer, but with less passion than Tasso and more interest in the lady's state of mind. *14. goodly.* Graciously.

25 (LXVIII). This Easter sonnet parallels the Lenten sonnet (**10**) of the previous year. From here to **32** the sonnets celebrate a happy betrothal.

3. having harrowed hell. Refers to Christ's entry into hell and release of its victims on the day after the crucifixion. *3–4. bring away captivity.* Recalling

Psalm cxxvi.4, 'Turn again our captivity'. The return of the Jewish captives from Babylon was taken to prefigure the harrowing of hell. *thence...win.* Then (on Easter day) to win us still on earth, captives to original sin. *9–12.* Turning from 'we' as mankind generally to 'we' as the poet and lady, here enjoined to base their lives on Christ's example. *weighing worthily.* Considering in suitable fashion. *11. like dear.* Souls equally dear (to Christ). *buy.* Redeem.

26 (LXX). Commemorating the second spring of courtship, and based on the traditional romance lyric in which the lover bids his lady wake and celebrate the rites of May. Cf. Wyatt 3.

1. Love's mighty king. Either Eros, or the 'May King' who presided over the rites: cf. **9**.3–4. *2. coat-armour.* Literally, coat embroidered with heraldic arms; here used figuratively for the meadows. *5. careless.* Without regard (for spring's coming). *8. by the forelock.* In Renaissance emblems, Opportunity was depicted as a woman with her head shaven except for a forelock: only by grasping this could one make her serve one's will. *11. make.* Mate, companion.

27 (LXXII). Suggested by Tasso's *Quell'alma ch'immortal*, which declared that the lady's soul, unsoiled by the body's vesture, soars heavenwards but returns out of pity for her mortal lovers. Here the lover's spirit, unable to ascend to heaven, finds heaven's bliss on earth.

2. in mind. With intention. *4. mortality.* Human life. *8.* 'And forgets her former (intended) flight to heaven'. *13. not with none.* (Emphatic double negative.)

28 (LXXIV). In honour of the 'three Elizabeths': his Mother, his Queen, and his lady, Elizabeth Boyle.

1. trade. handicraft; alluding to the elaborately traced capital 'E' in Elizabethan script or carving. *3. three times thrice happy.* Each Elizabeth has in her respective way made him 'thrice happy' (cf. **1**, **18**). *5, 7. kind...kind.* The identical rhyming word, but signifying (1) nature; (2) gracious. *8. large richesse.* In 1591, after the publication of the first three books of *The Faerie Queene*, Spenser received a pension of £50 from the Queen; he had already been granted an estate at Kilcolman in Ireland. *lent.* Granted. *13. Ye three Elizabeths.* Perhaps suggesting the biblical 'three Marys'. *14. graces.* The 'Elizabeths' are finally associated with the classical Graces, who delighted the hearts of gods and men.

29 (LXXVI). Forming with **30** a double sonnet, expanded from Tasso's *Non son sì belli*, in praise of his lady's bosom. Spenser shifts his attention from Tasso's almost pagan delight in physical beauty to his own thoughts whose sensuousness is qualified by affirmations of beauty's spiritual origins and virtuous influence. For a detailed comparison see Lever, 110–13.

1, 4. virtue's...sprite. Spiritual epithets replacing Tasso's comparisons to spring flowers and autumn fruit, fostered by Love and Nature. *3.* Recalling the Bower of Bliss and Garden of Adonis in *The Faerie Queene* II.xii and III.vi. *5. ravished.* Transported in rapture. *6. my frail thoughts.* Dissociated from the essential 'I'. *7. insight.* 'Inner eye', in contrast to physical sight. *13.* While Tasso's 'bold thought' (*audace pensier*) cannot be restrained, Spenser's thoughts enjoy 'happy rest'.

30 (LXXVII). Based on Tasso's sestet; Spenser's 'golden apples' are not pagan, but brought from paradise, as Love's projection of spiritual beauty in a world of nature.

2. a goodly table. The lady's bosom. *3. junkets.* Dainties. *4. the greatest prince.* (1) A temporal ruler; (2) God as King of kings. *6. unvalued.* Invaluable. *7.* One of the twelve labours of Hercules was to fetch the golden apples of the Hesperides. *8.* Atalanta was required to marry the first man to outmatch her in running. Her suitor dropped three golden apples in her way; 'enticed' to pick these up, she was overtaken by him in the race.

31 (LXXX). Refers to the completion of Books IV–VI of *The Faerie Queene*, published in 1596 (cf. **13**).

3. half foredone. Half completed (Spenser planned to write twelve books). *6. prison.* Self-imposed restraint. *7. that second work.* The second half of the poem. *9. pleasant mew.* Happy confinement. *10. sport.* Recreate. *13–14.* The Faery Queen was identified, in Spenser's letter to Raleigh, with Queen Elizabeth, before whom the lady could only have the status of 'handmaid'.

32 (LXXXIV).

6. well-tempered sprites. Spirits or souls whose composition (of humours) is well balanced. (Cf. **7**.4.) *9–10. yourself...myself.* The distinction between the poet's 'thoughts' and his entire person recalls **29**.6. *13–14. perfection...election.* Each is pronounced as a word of four syllables. *14. election.* Choice, with Calvinist overtones suggesting preordained divine favour.

33 (LXXXVI). A fierce denunciation of some slanderer whose lies have angered the lady. From here to the end of the sequence the sonnets express doubt and deprivation.

1. Since the adder was popularly believed to poison with its tongue, it symbolized slander. *2. the Furies.* Latin *Furiae*, avenging spirits. Identified here with Gorgons, female spirits whose heads were crowned with serpents. *8. coals of ire.* Anger. *10. head.* Referring back to the 'heads' of ll. 2–3. *12.* Intending to have caused a 'breach' between the poet and his lady.

34 (LXXXVIII). Composed in absence from the lady.

1. comfort. Guidance. *2. astray.* In the direction of love; cf. **29**.6. *6. their shadows vain.* Their own insignificant images. *7. th'only image.* The unique likeness. *heavenly ray.* (from the lady's eyes.) *8. glance.* Gleam. *9–10.* Through examining his soul (*'purest part'*) he can conceive the Platonic 'idea' of heavenly beauty which for his eye is only a still-lingering gleam.

SAMUEL DANIEL

Twenty-eight of Daniel's sonnets first appeared in an appendix to Newman's unauthorised edition of Sidney's *Astrophel and Stella* (1591). In 1592 twenty-four of these, with additional poems, were published under the title *Delia*, together with the narrative poem *The Complaint of Rosamond*. The sonnets were reprinted with minor changes from 1592 to 1598, and were extensively revised in the collected edition of Daniel's *Works* (1601). The text here and numbering in brackets follow Sprague's edition (1930, 1950), which preferred the early texts to the revised versions; but the more important changes are mentioned in the notes.

1–5 (XXXI–XXXV). These sonnets are linked into a series by their last and first rhymes (a device used by Donne in his *La Corona* series).

1. Inspired by two stanzas of Tasso's *Gerusalemme Liberata* xvi which Spenser translated in *The Faerie Queene* ii.xii. 74–5. Tasso's theme is that the rose should be gathered while it is still in the bud, before it opens and dies.

1. Look, Delia. From Tasso's opening, *Deh, mira,* ('Ah, see',) introducing the song of a bird in the lovers' garden of Armida. *2. image.* Counterpart. *honour.* Adornment. *3–4.* Altered in 1601 to 'Whilst yet her tender bud doth undisclose That full of beautie, Time bestowes uppon her'. The influence of Shakespeare, Sonnet LIV has been suggested, but the themes are different, and resemblances appear only in such common words as 'buds', 'roses', 'discloses'. *8.* The image of the morning sun overcast by clouds has no counterpart in Tasso (or Spenser), but resembles *ShS* 15. *9.* From Tasso's *'nè, perchè faccia in dietro april ritorno, Si rinfiora ella mai, nè si rinverde'* ('Nor though the (flower's) face return in April, will it (mortal life) flower or grow green again'). *11.* The metre and alliteration beautifully suggest the grace of a flying figure. *feathered*: given wings. *14. again.* In return.

2

2–4. Emphasises and expands Tasso's injunction to love 'now'. *5–10.* Expanded from Tasso: *'Così trapassa nel trapassar d'un giorno De la vita mortale il fiore e'l verde'* ('So passes away with a day's passing the flower and verdure of mortal life'). *7. joy.* Enjoy. *sweet be done.* Pleasure be over. *11–12.* 'Believe that whatever will most hide and cover lowest your fading beauty will best suit it'. *13. weigh.* Estimate. *that.* What.

3

2. The long vowels, internal rhyme (*thou...brow*) and inverted stress (*sitting alone*) give the line a reflective poignancy that matches the opening of Ronsard's great sonnet, *'Quand vous serez bien vieille, au soir, à la chandelle, Assise auprès du feu.'* *4. tells the truth.* The first 1592 edition has 'tells thee trueth'. *5–8.* In Ronsard's sonnet the poet is dead by the time his ageing mistress, proud of the verse she once inspired, regrets her cruelty. Daniel is at once more modest and more sure of his own survival. *7. fadest.* Didst fade (repeats *thy fading,* **2.**11). *14. golden.* Altered in 1601 to 'sable'; cf. *ShS* 4.4: 'sable curls all silvered o'er'.

4

1–2. In 1601 *golden* is altered, as in **3.**14, to *sable,* and *flowers* to *beauties.* Cf. *ShS* **2.**7–8: 'Sap checked with frost...Beauty o'ersnowed and bareness everywhere'. *5. this picture.* Figurative for the description of Delia in verse. *6. Limned.* Applicable both to painting and to literary characterisation; similarly with *pencil,* as either a painter's brush or a writing implement. *all.* Entirely. *9.* Repeats the image of verse as an eternal monument from Horace and Ovid, but resembles *ShS* 22 in offering it to the beloved. *10. happily.* A common variant of 'haply'. *11. These colours.* In keeping with the 'picture' image of ll. 5–6.

5

1. zeal. Ardour. *abound.* Be at large. *2. conceive.* Sympathetically understand. *4. In base attire.* In the mean trappings of his verse. *5–6.* Cf. *AS* 5.5–7. *5. within.* The first 1592 edition has 'in'. The change is called for by the metre. *10. her flight.* (That of Delia's fame, personified in the traditional Roman winged figure *'fama'.)* *12. in an immortal style* (1) In a manner that would make her immortal; (2) in immortal verse. *13. limned.* Portrayed or described (as in **4.**6).

6 (XXXVI).

1. O be not grieved. Cf. *ShS* 17.1: 'No more be grieved'. *2. Bewray.* Reveal. *6. warble.* Song. *8. in ice.* At once perishable and frigid. *9–12.* Schaar (1) argues (32–33) that Daniel borrowed his imagery from Shakespeare Sonnet LXXXI. 5–8. If there was borrowing, the likelihood is that Daniel influenced Shakespeare. *10. reserved in pureness.* Preserved through their untainted sincerity. *11–12. redeemed…obscureness.* Delia's eyes (i.e. her beauty) have redeemed the poet from the life of common men, and in so doing have enabled *him* to save her from future obscurity. *13. careful.* Sorrowful.

7 (XXXVII).

1–4. An expansion of Ovid's *'iam seges est ubi Troia fuit'* ('Now there is a ploughed field where Troy once stood') (*Heroides* 1.i.53). *1. admireth.* The contemporary usage of singular verb-form with plural subject (similarly in l.7: *'actions…hath'*). *2. the which ambition.* Altered in 1601 to 'which proud ambition'. *3. check.* Curb. *entombed.* Covered with earth. *lien.* Lain. *4. eared.* An archaism for 'ploughed' (Old English *erian*, to plough). *6. spoil.* Reward. *7–8. gained…pen.* Found place in the everlasting records compiled by a worthy writer. *10. spoil.* Despoil. *veil.* Outer, physical form. *11. mortality.* Mortal men. *12.* Schaar (2) found the source of this difficult line in the early version of a sonnet by Bernardino Rota. This contains the eulogy *'tu nata a scettro, a regno, Tra le stelle alzerai l'ago, e la gonna'* ('You, born to the sceptre and to rule, will raise amongst the stars the needle and the mantle'). *trail.* (As a lady's train and also a train of light—as a shooting star—this makes a happy rendering of *gonna*.) *13. t'in-woman.* To embody in woman's form. Schaar shows that the verb was based on a mistranslation of Rota's *se'ndonna* ('gains mastery of'), which Daniel took to mean 'makes into a woman'.

8 (XXXVIII). The opening conceit with its tragic overtones turns into a hopeful variation on the Petrarchan 'galley' metaphor.

1–2. Alludes to the Greek legend of the young lover Leander who was drowned while swimming across the Hellespont to visit his mistress Hero. *1. Fair.* Changed to 'Most faire' in 1601. *3. forspent.* Worn out, exhausted. (Altered to 'quite spent' after the first edition.) *6. convoy.* Ship under escort. *7. virtue.* Special merit or accomplishment. *10. darts so right.* Shoots so accurately. (In keeping with l. 9, the conventional association of 'darts' with 'eyes' is changed to 'darts-hand'.) *11.* The mention of old resentments is much toned down in the 1594 revision: 'I shall forget olde wrongs, my griefs shall cease'. *13. Once let the ocean* was changed in 1594 to 'O let th'Ocean'.

9 (XL).

1–4. The conceit of tears stirred like the sea's tides resembles Donne's in *A Valediction: Of Weeping:* 'O more than Moone, Draw not up seas to drowne me in thy sphere'. *1. Cynthia.* The classical moon goddess. Altered to 'DELIA' in 1594. *2. attending.* In attendance, like a queen's ladies-in-waiting. Changed in 1601 to 't'attend' (with 'end' for *ending*, l. 4) to avoid 'feminine' rhymes. *3.* Editions from 1594–8 change *nor ever dries* to 'but ever rise'. *6. his sovereign's course.* The moon's course through the sky is identified with an Elizabethan royal 'progress'. *7. impost.* Tribute. *9–10.* The moon-sea conceit changes into a new image where Delia becomes a rock against which the sea of the poet's tears beats in vain. *10. zeal.* (As in **5**.1.) *fury.* Fierce passion, seen as the gale stirring the waves. *12. joy.* Enjoy. *13–14.* Altered in 1601 to 'And if I finde such pleasure to complaine, What should I do then if I should obtaine?' *14. in compass of.* In the bounds of.

10 (XLII).

2. refresh. Action of refreshing. *3. but.* Only. *7. nourish.* Cherish. *9. surcharged.* Weighed down. *10. bend.* Incline. *11–12.* Changed in 1601 to 'And that in Beauties lease expir'd, appears The date of age...' The 'lease' image may have been suggested by *ShS* 5.5, 'that beauty which you hold in lease', and 9.4, 'And summer's lease hath all too short a date'. *11. a passport for thy fears.* A free pass for the things you fear to proceed into effect. *12. age...death.* The calends in Roman and later reckoning were the first day of the new month; old age is thus seen as the first onset of death. *13. this hath been often told.* Changed in 1601 to 'this must not be fore-told'.

11 (XLV). An invocation of sleep, as in *AS* 18, Drummond 4, and *Caelica* 4.
1. Care-charmer. Subduer or soother of cares. *2. Brother to death.* (A proverbial description.) *6. ill-adventured.* Badly provided for its voyage: a conceit suggested by the merchant adventurers' expeditions of the time. *7. their scorn.* The scorn in which they are held. *9. imagery.* Mental images (cf. *Caelica* 4, 'images of self-confusednesses'). *11. approve.* Prove. *13. embracing clouds in vain.* Perhaps a reminiscence of the myth of Endymion, the sleeping shepherd beloved by the moon.

12 (XLVI).
1–2. Alluding to Spenser's *Faerie Queene*, Books I–III of which appeared in 1590. The opening theme, in the form 'let others sing of heroes, my verse shall praise only you', derived from an Anacreontic ode imitated by Ronsard and others (Schaar 1). *1. paladins.* Originally knights of Charlemagne, whose feats were versified by Ariosto and other Italian poets; but serving as a general term for knights errant. *2. aged...words.* Archaic stresses and obsolete diction (as used by Spenser). *3. shadows.* Symbols. *lines.* Lines of verse and painted features. *6.* 'My verse...shall vouch for the genuine beauty (of your eyes).' Cf. *ShS* 8.1: 'Who will believe my verse in time to come'. *7. lo where she lies*. A common formula in elegies. *9. the arks.* From the biblical ark of the covenant that accompanied the Israelites in the desert and gave them divine protection against their enemies. *trophies.* Memorials of victory. *12. time's consuming rage.* Suggested by Ovid's *tempus edax rerum, tuque invidiosa vetustas,* ('Time, devourer of things, and you, jealous age'). *13–14.* Weakened in the 1601 version: 'Though th'error of my youth in them appeare, Suffice they shew I liv'd and lov'd thee deare'.

MICHAEL DRAYTON

Fifty-one sonnets of Drayton were first published as *Idea's Mirror* in 1594. The sequence, re-named *Idea*, underwent successive revisions from 1599 to 1619. Many early sonnets were omitted, some revised, and others added as Drayton worked towards a distinctive style. The text and order here are based on Hebel's edition of Drayton's works, and follow the 1619 edition.

1. Headed 'To the Reader of these Sonnets'. Added in 1599 as a disclaimer of the affected style ridiculed by the satirists Hall, Marston and others.

1. passion. Passionate speech (cf. *ShS* 11.2 and note.) *2. turning other books.* Echoes *AS* 1.7, 'Oft turning others' leaves'. *4. his labour satisfy.* Reward his efforts. *7. 'ah me's'.* Marston derided 'ay me's' in *The Scourge of Villainy* (1598). *8. libertine.* One who goes his own way. *fantastically.* Following fancy. *12. sportively.* In light fashion. *13-14.* The English style of dress was notoriously a medley of continental fashions (see Portia's remarks on 'the young baron of England', *Merchant of Venice* i.ii). The 1599 version of l. 13, 'My active muse is of the world's right strain', was less topical and more vaguely moralistic.

2 (i). Based on the Petrarchan image of love as a ship in storm (cf. Wyatt 2, etc.); but Drayton's main concern is with the varied experiences of Elizabethan voyagers. Cf. Donne, 'Let sea-discoverers to new worlds have gone' (*The Good-Morrow*).

3. his discovery. What he discovered. *8.* How the altitude of the north star was taken (as a guide to navigation); cf. *ShS* 39. 7-8. *9. doubled.* sailed round.

3 (ii). The romance conceit of the 'slain heart' is developed into a crime story.

1. none...I. 'Only you and I were present.' *2. should.* Could. *5. on the view.* On formal examination (as at an inquest). *6. quit.* Acquit. *8. so great a proof.* Such great weight. *11.* Suggested by Sidney's conceit of Cupid as a mischievous boy hiding in the ambush of the lady's eye, *AS* 10.

4 (v). The wordplay turns on the Elizabethan spelling of 'Ay' as 'I', here modernised.

4. affirming No, denying Ay. Denial in a tone of acceptance (ll. 6, 8), affirmation in a tone of denial (ll. 5, 7). *5. slightly.* Slightingly. The 1619 edn. has 'sleightly', i.e. craftily; this is rather unfitting to the sense of l. 4. *6. pule.* Whine. *7. echo.* (Repeating the vowel, not the word.) *10. No I am I.* 'I am not truly a person (or man)'. *13-14.* 'Substitute yourself ("I") for the "Ay", and give yourself with the word "No" '.

5 (vi). The easy hyperbole of this 'immortalization' may be contrasted to Shakespeare's earnest approach.

1. things. Women (with contempt). *2. coaches.* Increasingly fashionable for court ladies. (In *AS* 41, Stella is glimpsed in a coach by Astrophel.) *8.* Upon surplus praises cast away as alms for queens.

6 (xi). A remarkable treatment of the theme of interchanged selves, which brings out the lover's ambivalent craving, both for union and for separateness. The sonnet looks ahead to the lovers' parting in **12**.

3. 'Since you were fully a person to me, I have lost my own personality.' *5-6.* Cf. Shakespeare, *Phoenix and Turtle*: 'Hearts remote, yet not asunder, Distance, and no space was seen...To themselves yet either neither'. *8. absent.* i.e. from the normal world of themselves. *9-10.* Drayton's desire for human separation may be compared with Donne's for divine union, *HS* 10.12-14. See Introd., pp. 17-18.

7 (xv). First printed in 1619, and entitled 'His Remedy for Love'. The gaily cynical recipe, suggesting ingredients of black magic, assembles far-fetched conceits of rarity in the manner of Donne's *Song* 'Go and catch a falling star'.

1. stead. Help. *3. her.* Such a woman's. (Similarly in ll. 5 and 7.) *8.* Suggested perhaps by the tale of the widow of Ephesus in Petronius' *Satiricon*. She was soon won by a handsome soldier at her husband's tomb. *13. to win me.* i.e. from love. (Cf. 'You do bewitch me', **6.**13.)

8 (xvii). First printed in 1594, but much worked over and completely revised for the 1619 edn. Entitled 'To Time'. The idea of the beloved as an embodiment of earth's pristine beauty parallels *ShS* LXVIII, 'Thus is his cheek the map of days outworn'.

4. 'In whom heaven sees itself mirrored'. *5. tralucent.* Translucent: emitting light. *7. his.* Its (the world's). *11. nephews.* Descendants. *14.* Refers not to the mistress's present death, but to Time's awareness of it at some future date.

9 (xix). Entitled 'To Humour'. An attractive use of natural speech-rhythms and colloquial terms, in the manner of Sidney (cf. *AS* 29.12–14).

9. shift. Evasion. *10. coil.* Fuss, ado. *14. You...hate.* 'You make hate a stratagem of love.'

10 (xxiii). Developed, like *AS* 5, from a popular anacreontic conceit.

9. for. In return for. *9–12.* Love's treacherous enticement of the poet's thoughts is closer to the traditional theme than Sidney's indulgent version where the damage—both to the lover and to Love—is unintended.

11 (xxiv). Suggested by *AS* LIV: ' "What, he," say they of me; "No, I dare swear/He cannot love..." '

3. The lightness of his verse—announced in advance in **1**—will prove that he is not in love. *7. in sport.* 'Diverting myself'. *8. conceit.* Supposition. *9. censures.* Criticisms. (Perhaps 'censors', i.e. critics, is meant.) *10. pleasant.* Jesting. *11.* 'Where only by death is fame to be got.'

12 (LI). This has been compared to *ShS* 34 as an account of outstanding events in recent years. But Drayton is far more specific and topical; Shakespeare's references—if meant to be non-figurative—have remained too obscure, or cryptic, to be dated.

4. As't. The 1605 edn. has 'As', which reads more smoothly. *5–9.* Essex's downfall and execution were in February 1601; Tyrone's Irish army was decisively beaten before Kinsale in December 1602; the Queen died quietly on 24 March 1603, and James VI of Scotland journeyed to London in April. Peace with Spain and the Spanish Netherlands was signed on 18 August 1604, thus ending the alliance with the Dutch.

13 (LIX). Entitled 'To Proverb'. The exchange of proverbs may have been suggested by a dialogue in Florio's *Second Fruits* (1591). Sidney's sonnets contain conversations between the poet and a personified Love, and quick repartees as in *AS* 17.

1. harboured. Lodged. *4. again.* In answer. Love's proverb here seems less a reply to that of l. 3 than a statement countered in l. 5. *5. speed.* Prosper. *6.* Ambiguous; as an answer to l. 5, this would mean 'You will do no better being forward than being slow'. *11. the by.* The secondary or minor consideration. *12.* 'You have talked well about nothing. . .'.

14 (LXI). First printed in 1619. This fine dramatic monologue is related to the experience treated in **6**, and the conclusion is inherent in the relationship itself. (See Introd., p. 18). The tone expresses, as often in Donne, a love between equals, based on an understanding deeper than love. Formally the sonnet has a typically English simplicity and restraint, with an imaginative intensity in the sestet that recalls the Italian tradition.

2. you...me. Perhaps an unconscious echo of Chaucer's identical phrase in *The Squire's Tale* 343. *10. passion speechless lies.* As in **1**.1, *passion* implies 'passionate speech'.

WILLIAM SHAKESPEARE

Shakespeare's Sonnets were published, apparently without authority, by Thomas Thorpe in 1609. Here the numbering in brackets and text (except where changes are indicated) follows Thorpe's Quarto. Numbers **1–46** are addressed to an unnamed friend, **47–56** to an unidentified mistress. See Introd., pp. 18–19.

1 (II).

1. forty. Used in the bible for a large number; also the time-span of a generation. *winters.* Humanised through *besiege* as enemy troops. *2. trenches.* Wrinkles. *3. livery.* Distinctive garb. *4. tattered weed.* (Quarto 'totter'd', a spelling variant). (1) ragged clothing (cf. *proud livery,* l. 3); (2) valueless plant (cf. *beauty's field*), l. 2). *7. deep sunken.* Suggesting the miser's buried treasure. *8. all eating.* (Since such treasure will be 'eaten' by the grave.) *9. use.* Gainful employment; as often, in the sense of procreation. *11. sum my count.* Render my account. *excuse.* Justification.

2 (V).

1. hours. The personification stems from *Horae* in Latin mythology, meaning 'seasons'; hence the winter-summer images from l. 5 on. *2. gaze.* Object gazed at. *3. play the tyrants.* A stock figure, derived from such morality-play 'tyrants' as Herod or Cambises. *4. Unfair.* Makes ugly. *5–6.* The change of seasons in time is transposed to a change of place, involving military defeat; a development from **1**.1–2. *9–10.* Suggested by Sidney's image in *Arcadia* of rosewater preserved in a glass as a description of marriage. During the annihilation of summer's beauty, the distilled flower of progeny survives in a glass-like womb. *11. Beauty's effect with beauty.* The sensuous impression together with beauty itself. *12. no remembrance.* ('would remain' is implied.) *14. Leese.* Lose. Shakespeare did not use this variant elsewhere; it might be merely the Quarto's misreading of 'Loose' (i.e. Lose).

3 (VII). The sun-king image is developed from Helios in classical mythology, a divine ruler drawn in his chariot across the sky.

1. the orient. With Renaissance associations of riches and splendour; Helios rose daily from his magnificent palace in the eastern sky. *gracious.* (1) regal or sovereign; (2) emitting and bestowing beauty; and (3) 'spriritually beneficent' (Ingram and Redpath). *2. under.* On earth. *5. steep-up heavenly hill.* The sun's sphere in Ptolemaic astronomy. *6.* (With maximum strength in mid-course.) *13. thyself outgoing.* Passing beyond your prime. *14. a son.* The wordplay on 'sun' clinches the metaphor. (The begetting of a son was of major importance where estates and a title were involved.)

4 (XII). Re-working the themes of **2–3**. On the verse structure see Booth, 64–84.

1–4. The range expands from minutes-hours to day-night, to seasons, and to the human life-span. Alliteration and assonance heighten the effect. *2. brave.* Resplendent. *4. all silvered o'er.* Quarto has 'ore siluer'd ore', possibly wordplay on 'or' (gold) and 'o'er' (over); but 'gold' contradicts *sable* curls. An alternative reading is 'o'er-silvered all'. *7. girded up.* Applicable both to sheaves and to a human figure belted or girdled. *8.* The end of summer and of a man's life are fused in the harvest image through the implied presence of 'Death the reaper', who appears in l. 13. *9. question make.* Raise as a theme for reflection. *10. the wastes of time.* Cf. **2.**5–6. *11. themselves forsake.* Depart from their own nature. *14. brave.* Defy; in counterpoise to *the brave day sunk*, l. 2.

5 (XIII).
1. yourself. As a unique personality. *love.* The first use of this endearment. In this sonnet the friend is also for the first time addressed as 'you'. *3. this coming end.* (There is no mention of an afterlife.) *6. determination.* Cessation in the legal sense. The lease conceit is a variant on the image of life as a loan from nature. *7. Yourself...your self's.* Distinguishing the perpetuated identity from the transient self of one life-span. (Quarto prints 'your self' as two words throughout.) *9–12.* An image from Erasmus, *In Praise of Marriage*: 'It lieth in your hands to keep that house from decay, whereof you're lineally descended' (tr. Thomas Wilson, *The Art of Rhetoric*, 1553). *10. husbandry.* (1) Domestic economy; (2) the husband's sexual function. *12.* Cf. *Delia* 12.12: 'Against the dark, and time's consuming rage.' *14. You had a father.* (i.e. The friend's father is already dead.)

6 (XIV).
1. my judgment pluck. Snatch or steal my knowledge (of the future, as in almanacs and prognostications). *2. astronomy.* Astrology. *4. seasons' quality.* Good or bad seasons for crops. *5. to brief minutes.* Minute by minute. *6. Pointing ...his...* Appointing to each (minute) its... *8. oft predict.* frequent prediction. *10. constant stars.* Fixed stars in the Ptolemaic heaven. The traditional euphemism for the eyes of the beloved serves an astrological conceit on the friend's mutability. *11. truth.* A new attribute of the friend, coupled with his beauty. *12.* Farming imagery: 'If you would keep aside part of yourself as breeding stock'. *14.* Truth and beauty are not Platonic ideas but aspects of personality. See Introd., p. 20.

7 (XV). The astrological conceit of **6** is now blended with previous images of time and transiency.
3. this huge stage. Not only the traditional figure ('All the world's a stage') but suggesting the Elizabethan theatre with its tiers of spectators like stars in their spheres and its stage canopy, 'the heavens'. *4. in secret influence comment.* Like spectators, the stars comment on the 'shows'; they also exercise an unseen influence on the actors (*influence* as the mysterious astral power shaping the character and fate of sublunary beings). *6. Cheered and checked.* Relating both to an audience's response and the action of seasons and stars. *7. at height decrease.* Like the sun, **3.**9–10; which evokes the metaphor of l. 12. *8. brave state.* Fine attire; as in the clothing images of **1.**3–4. *14.* Immortality in verse is for the first time put forward as an alternative to perpetuation by breed. *engraft.* Set into another stock; i.e. give new life through poetry.

8 (XVII).
2. deserts. (Rhyming with *parts*, l. 4.) *6. in...number.* Enumerate in new verse.

8. touches...touched. Strokes of the pen...related to. *11. a poet's rage.* Wild, vatic outpouring; 'furor poeticus'. *12. stretched.* Strained, stilted. *antique.* (Interchangeable with 'antic'); both ancient and fantastic.

9 (XVIII).

3. darling buds. The vulnerable beauty of the flowers is humanised and made lovable, while their function of reproduction is no longer suggested. *4. summer's lease.* Fusing the legal and seasonal imagery of previous sonnets. *8. untrimmed.* To 'trim' is to adjust sails when facing an adverse wind; beauty cannot adjust itself to *nature's changing course*, and so *declines...untrimmed.* The octave ends in finely balanced alliterative effects. *9.* Eternal summer is equated to the unfading flower (as against the intemperate season and exposed buds of 1-3); both typify the friend. *10.* Implying beauty held in perpetual lease (in contrast to l. 4). *12. eternal lines.* With wordplay on *lines* (1) of verse; (2) as features (lineaments).

10 (XIX).

1. Devouring Time. Ovid's *tempus edax rerum* (*Metamorphoses* xv). *blunt thou the lion's paws*: From Ovid's *Tristia* IV: *tempore paenorum compescitur ira leonum. 4.* The phoenix was reputed to live for at least five hundred years, and thereafter to burn itself to death. *5. fleets.* Quarto 'fleet'st' spoils the rhyme, and its harsh suffix '-tst' was usually avoided by Shakespeare. *10. antic.* Quarto 'antique', with two meanings (see note to **8**.12). Here stress and context suggest the sense 'grotesque' rather than 'ancient'. *11. course.* (Cf. **9**.8.)

11 (XX). Often misinterpreted, through misunderstanding of Elizabethan idioms, and ignorance of the romance tradition generally. Half serious, half playful, the sonnet in fact disclaims physical homosexuality.

2. the master mistress...passion. 'The man addressed in the style of a sonnet mistress, who is the subject of my impassioned speech.' The oxymoron 'master mistress' is typical of Shakespeare. 'Passion' was emotional rhetoric, or strong emotion, but there is no record of its use for 'sexual desire' before 1641 (*OED*). *4. false woman's fashion.* The false fashion of womankind. *5. rolling.* Turning in different directions. *6.* Cf. **15**.4. *7.* 'A man in form, exercising power over all forms or complexions (male and female)'. Quarto prints 'Hews' in italics, suggesting wordplay on 'hue' as (1) form; (2) complexion. *8. which.* Referring to *hue* (l. 7). *amazeth.* Perplexes, overwhelms with wonder. *12. one thing... nothing.* 'Thing' was a colloquialism for the sexual organ. The friend's maleness baffles any hope of treating him as a woman. *13-14.* 'Since nature marked you out with a prick to please women, let *me* have your love and let *them* treasure the sexual use you make of it.' To 'prick out' has the punning sense of (1) choose; (2) endow with a penis.

12 (XXVII). Unlike *AS* 18, and other romance treatments of the beloved seen in dreams, since here the waking imagination projects the vision. See Introd., p. 21.

2. travel. Quarto 'trauaill'. The spellings for 'travail' and 'travel' were interchangeable, but the latter meaning seems primary here. *4. work my mind.* Keep my mind active. *6. Intend.* Prepare to make. *9. soul's imaginary sight.* Mind's eye, functioning through imagination. *10. thy.* Quarto 'their' is kept by some modern editors, as referring to *thoughts*, l. 5; but this noun is too far from the pronoun for the sense to be clear. Also 'their shadow' is vague, *thy shadow* explicit and forceful. *11. like a jewel hung in ghastly night.* The image of light seen in darkness is re-worked in a new context in **25**.14. *14. For thee... myself.* 'On account of you and my own imagination.'

13 (XXIX). Mental distress and emotional turmoil strain the metrical pattern of the octave and find release in the imagery of the sestet.

1. in disgrace...eyes. Deserted by grace, metaphysical and social (*men's eyes*). *2. I all alone.* Phonetic effects and impeded metre reflect the intensely subjective mood. *outcast state.* Alienation from the cosmos and other men. *3. trouble deaf heaven.* The metrical disturbance corresponds to that in l. 2. *5. one more rich in hope.* Probably not alluding to a particular person: the developed idea in l. 7 refers to acquaintances in general. *8. enjoy.* Possess. *9–14.* For a description of the verse technique, see Booth, 48–9. *11–12.* The image seems to come from a verse in Du Bartas, reprinted in Eliot's *Ortho-epia* (1593): '*La gentile Alouëtte...vire vers la voute du Ciel...et desire dire, adieu Dieu, adieu Dieu*'. Lyly described the lark in *Campaspe* v.i. 'How at heaven's gates she claps her wings'. Cf. *Cymbeline* II.3: 'Hark, hark! the lark at heaven's gate sings'.

14 (XXX). Terms from law and accountancy—*sessions, waste, dateless, cancelled, expense, tell, account, pay, losses*—pervade the sonnet.

1. sessions. Suggesting 'an enquiry in a manorial court...into the condition of the estate' (Ingram and Redpath). *4. with...wail.* Grieve again at old causes of grief. *10. tell.* Count.

15 (XXXIII). Analogous images in the history plays are pointed out by Lever, 221–3 and Mahood, *Shakespeare Survey* 15, 50–3. The sun as a figure of mutability appears in **3, 7** and **9**: here it points up the antinomies of being-seeming, truth-falsehood.

1. glorious. Resplendent (like the sun), renowned (like a king). *2. Flatter.* Praise, compliment. *4.* The association of sunshine and alchemy appears in the plays in contexts of betrayal (e.g. *King John* III.i.77–80). *5. basest.* Lowest, and also darkest. *8. disgrace.* Cf. **13**.1. *12. region cloud.* The middle region of the air in which clouds are formed. *stain.* (1) Suffer eclipse; (2) become corrupted.

16 (XXXIV). In effect a dramatic monologue, where the presumed responses of the person addressed form part of the poem.

1. The figure changes from the sun's 'disgrace' to the traveller's, deceived by his trust. *3. base clouds.* Repeating *basest clouds*, **15**.5. *4. bravery.* Applicable to the sun's splendour and a king's robes. *rotten smoke.* Unwholesome mist. *7–8.* The veiled allusions are to some apology or compensation offered without true restitution. The imagery contrasts mere closing of a wound to a complete cure. *speak.* Rhyming with *break*, l. 5. *12. cross.* Generally accepted for Quarto 'losse' which repeats the rhyme ending of l. 10. *13–14.* 'He finds the spectacle of love "in tears" irresistible...he goes on in XXXV [17] to forgive, to find excuses, and even to blame himself as an "accessary" ' (Dover Wilson).

17 (XXXV). The friend's treachery is condoned as but one instance of a universal corruption.

1–4. Recurrent images of duality. *5. in this.* In excusing the friend's fault by reference to those of *all men*. *7. salving thy amiss.* (Like the ineffective 'salve' offered by the friend, **16**.7.) *8. thy.* Generally adopted for Quarto 'their'. *are.* Are excused. *9–11.* He has justified the friend's *sensual fault* by *sense*—the ways of the sensory, phenomenal world—thus condoning the moral sin he should condemn, and undermining his own claim to have been wronged. *13. accessary.* Neither advocate nor prosecutor, but an accessary to the crime. *14. sweet thief.* (The 'theft' seems to be that referred to in **19** and **49**).

18 (XXXVI). A separation imposed by social expediency.
3. those blots. Deliberately obscure, but probably connected with the 'stain' of **15**.14 and **17**.3. *5. respect.* Regard. *6. separable spite.* Hostility requiring a separation. *9. acknowledge.* Publicly greet (this would include dedications of works). *10.* Even assumption of blame by the writer would compromise the friend. *14.* If the friend's reputation (*report*) is unimpaired, the poet will vicariously share it.

19 (XLI). The courtly excuses for the friend's misconduct in ll. 1–8 change to frank reproach in ll. 9–14.
1. pretty. With undertones of the sense 'gallant'. *liberty.* Freedom from control. *3. befits.* Singular verb with plural subject; a common usage. *5. Gentle.* Ambiguous: (1) high-born; (2) easily dominated. *8. till he have prevailed.* 'She' for *he* is to be expected, but the male sexual response calls for *he*. The veiled inconsistency suggests where the poet mentally lays the blame. *9. seat.* Place where one claims possession or ownership; here, the poet's physical rights as lover. (Cf. *Othello* II.1: 'the lustful Moor Hath leaped into my seat'.)

20 (XLIX).
1. Against. In readiness for. *3. cast...sum.* Completed his check of the accounts rendered by the poet as steward (i.e. taken cognizance of the poet's behaviour). *4. advised respects.* Fully considered reasons. *8. settled gravity.* Fixed, unalterable weightiness. *9. ensconce me.* Take shelter. *11.* 'And raise my hand in oath against my own interests'; cf. **17**.10–11. *12. the lawful reasons.* A conceit explained in ll. 13–14.

21 (LII). Written in a period of separation.
1. key. Pronounced as a rhyme with *survey*, l. 3. *4. For.* For fear of. *8. captain.* Principal. *9–10. chest...wardrobe.* Similes for *the time that keeps you*. *12. imprisoned.* (Developed from the chest-wardrobe images: 'wardrobe' suggests 'ward', hence 'prison'.) *pride.* (1) Splendid adornment; (2) distinguished prisoner. *14. triumph.* Rejoice.

22 (LV). A sonnet of assertion and triumph without reservations or inner conflict. Inspired by the last of Horace's *Odes* (III.xxx) and the peroration of Ovid's *Metamorphoses* (xv.871ff.), it carries a like quality of finality.
1–8. Cf. Horace, *exegi monumentum aëre perennius, | regalique situ pyramidum altius* ('I have completed a monument more enduring than brass and higher than the royal building of pyramids'), and Ovid, *iamque opus exegi quod nec Iovis ira nec ignis | nec poterit ferrum nec edax abolere vetustas* ('My work is complete, which neither Jove's anger nor fire nor sword shall destroy, nor consuming age'). *1. monuments.* Quarto 'monument'. *2. powerful.* With power to commemorate its subject. *3.* (A recurrent image of the sonnets, not found in the Latin source; cf. **12**.11–12, **25**.14.) *7. Mars his sword.* i.e. the sword of Mars ('shall destroy' understood). *quick.* Fierce, eager. *9. all-oblivious.* Bringing all into oblivion. Quarto 'all oblivious' gives a weaker sense. *10. pace forth.* (Like

a soldier going into battle.) *find room.* Occupy a place. Perhaps with wordplay on 'Rome' (pronounced 'room'); i.e. 'Your praise shall carry Rome with it', recalling the same passage from Ovid. See Lever, 269–71. *12. wear...out.* Outlast this (transient) world. *ending doom.* Last Judgement.

23 (LX). See Lever, 252–5.

1–4. Cf. Ovid, *Metamorphoses* XV: *ut unda impellitur unda, / urgueturque eadem veniens urguetque priorem, / tempora sic fugiunt pariter pariterque sequuntur* ('as wave is driven on by wave, and, itself pursued, pursues the one before, so the moments of time at once flee and follow' (tr. Innes). *3. changing place.* Rising as the previous wave subsides. *5. Nativity.* Birth, personified as an infant. Cf. Ovid: *editus in lucem iacuit sine viribus infans* ('the baby, brought forth into the light, lies strengthless'). *Once...light.* 'When once it reaches the expanse of sky'. *main* usually meant 'sea', but is here caught up in the imagery of sunrise. *6. crowned.* The infant's growth is associated with the sun's mounting to its zenith and a royal heir's accession to the throne. *7.* The eclipses, like the waves and minutes, are humanised. Their *crooked* (sickle-shaped) invasion of the sun's disk shows the perverse malice of rebels or usurpers. *glory.* (1) Splendour of light; (2) royal fame; (3) personal honour. *9–12.* Time is an old churl with a spade or scythe. *9–10.* Cf. **1**.2. *transfix.* Cut or pierce through. *flourish.* Bloom. (*Youth* is thus a plant cut through by Time's spade). *11. rarities...truth.* Truth is a rare titbit for Time. *12. stands.* Applicable both to plants and men. *13. in hope.* Still hoped for.

24 (LXIV).
1. Time's fell hand. Cf. *his cruel hand,* **23**.14. *2. rich proud cost.* Resplendent, costly finery. *4. mortal.* (1) Pertaining to men; (2) death-dealing. *5–8.* From Ovid's instances of eternal mutability: *Vidi ego quod fuerat quondam solidissima tellus / esse fretum, vidi factas ex aequore terras* ('I myself have seen what was once solid earth changed into sea, and lands formed out of the main') *Metamorphoses* XV. This is linked through *hungry,* l. 5, to the Ovidian *tempus edax,* 'devouring time', and fused with Shakespeare's political-dramatic imagery through *gain Advantage* and *kingdom,* ll. 6–7. *9–10. interchange of state...state itself.* 'State' is (1) 'natural conditions'; (2) political *status quo*; involving (3) pomp and splendour. *14. that* i.e. *my love* (l. 12).

25 (LXV).
1–2. Summing up the observations of **24**. *2. sad.* Intent, resolute. *o'ersways.* Overrules. *3–4.* The legal metaphors *plea, action,* are fused with the natural images *beauty, flower,* as in **9**. *5–6.* Military figures are juxtaposed to *summer's honey breath,* the 'flower' of l. 4. While beauty vainly appeals to the law, Time attacks with his *battering days. 10.* In antithesis to **21**.9, *chest* now suggests not a preservative of life but a coffin. *14.* Cf. **12**.11–12.

26 (LXXI). One of a group of sonnets anticipating the poet's own death.
4. vilest. Quarto 'vildest', a common spelling variant, adds alliterative force. *8. make you woe.* Cause you grief. *11. rehearse.* Say over. *13. the wise world.* (With gentle irony.)

27 (LXXIII). See discussions by Ransom and Mizener (excerpts reprinted in *Shakespeare's Sonnets,* ed. Herrnstein, 102, 138–40); also Booth, 118–30.
4. Bare ruined choirs. Trees in autumn blend with a vision of post-Reformation

abbeys. (An example of 'soft-focus' impressionism, as against the hard, sequential imagery of metaphysical verse.) *ruined*. Quarto 'rn'wd'. *8. seals*. The Quarto spelling; but this may signify 'seels', a term from falconry for stitching up the eyes of a hawk in training. *9-12*. 'Wasting away on the ashes which once nourished it with living flame' (Dowden).

28 (LXXIV).

1. contented when. The colon that editors insert after *contented* is mistaken. As in **26** the question is how the friend should react 'after my death', not at the moment of reading this sonnet. *that fell arrest*. Cf. 'this fell serjeant Death / Is strict in his arrest', *Hamlet* v.ii.328-9. *3-4*. '*this line*' is a bequest; not a 'lump sum' enjoyed once, but a permanent income of love left for the friend. *4. memorial*. Reminder. *6*. i.e. *My spirit*, l. 8. *8. the better part of me*. Echoing Ovid, *Metamorphoses* XV: *Parte tamen meliore mei*. (While Ovid sees his 'better part' soaring above the stars, Shakespeare leaves it on earth, *consecrate to thee* (l. 6).) *11. a wretch's knife*. Possibly a weapon of Death personified, but Death is a serjeant of the law here, not an assassin. Shakespeare seems to have a specific risk in mind, and may well allude to the fatal knifing of Marlowe in 1593 by a secret agent in a Deptford tavern. *13. that*. His own body. *14. this*. His love, his verse, or both seen as one.

29 (LXXXVI). 'Giving two reasons why he has been reduced to silence, one genuine (ll. 1-4), the other (ll. 5-12) derisory' (Dover Wilson).

1. The friend as a theme for the rival poet resembles a treasure-laden ship attacked by a pirate. *5-6*. Chapman in his Induction to *The Tears of Peace* presented Homer's spirit, come to prompt the young English poet. Chapman had also written a continuation of the dead Marlowe's *Hero and Leander; that struck me dead* (l. 6), with '*me*' stressed, may imply that this sequel was as 'killing' to Shakespeare as the knife had been to Marlowe. *7. compeers by night*. Fellow-poets, who also might be nocturnal demons. (Chapman's early verse praised night and its ghostly visitants.) *9. that affable familiar ghost*. Inspiration helping like an intimate friend; but demonology is hinted at: a *familiar* was an evil attendant spirit. Burton (later) wrote of 'genii...very affable and familiar'. *10. gulls...intelligence*. (1) Deceives him with secret information; (2) makes him think he has exceptional understanding. *13. countenance*. (1) Beauty of features; (2) favour. *14*. Deliberate ambiguity; the friend's patronage of such a poet either made Shakespeare believe his own praises were now superfluous, or it weakened the case for praising the friend's merits.

30 (LXXXVII).

3-4. The figurative contract between poet and friend contains an escape clause; hence the poet's claims are legally terminated (*determinate*). *8. patent*. Exclusive right. *swerving*. Turning. *11. upon misprision growing*. Dependent upon a misunderstanding. *12. on...making*. Having formed a more correct opinion. *13-14*. (Like Sly the tinker in *The Taming of the Shrew*, persuaded in 'a flattering dream' that he is a great lord.)

31 (XCIV). Related to **16**, **19**, etc. on the friend's 'unkindness'. A much-disputed, ambivalent sonnet: see Booth's account (152-68) of critical opinions, and, for this editor's interpretation, Lever, 216-21. Ll. 1-8 are apparently a eulogy, but their opposite implications are brought out in the imagery of ll. 9-14.

1. Cf. Sidney's *Arcadia*: 'the more power he hath to hurt, the more admirable is his praise that he will not hurt'. Sidney's context is the tale of a young prince who seduced a married woman beloved by his father, but abandoned her out of filial respect. Shakespeare may have remembered this in connection with the triangular affair with the mistress. *2.* 'Who do not practise what is implied in their outward bearing.' *3. moving others.* (1) Stirring other people's emotional responses; (2) governing the actions of others (for good or ill). *3–4. as stone, Unmoved, cold.* Equivocal traits, deserving praise as compared with the *show* of unscrupulous sensuality, unpleasing as signs of perverse self-regard. The friend's decision to stay celibate may be due either to his being unmoved by temptation, or to his cold profligacy. Cf. Erasmus (tr. Wilson): 'such a one as hath no mind of marriage seemeth to be no man but rather a stone.' *6.* An uneasy reversal of the arguments for marriage in sonnets **1–9**, where 'to husband' meant to procreate, not hoard, and *expense* implied the waste of beauty in celibacy, not dissipation. *7.* Exercising rational control over their physical appeal. *8.* Recalls the *others* of l. 3, who do not govern the friend's reactions but only subserve him. *9–10. The summer's flower.* A recurrent image of vulnerable beauty. *to itself.* Unreproductive. As a celibate the friend may still grace his age; but if corrupted, he will be inferior to the commonest person (*The basest weed*) who reproduced his kind. *14.* Cf. Luke xii.27: 'Consider the lilies how they grow; they toil not, they spin not'. Symbolising celibate purity, the lily is superior to the rose or weed; but not if it festers.

32 (CIV). On the third anniversary of the first meeting with the friend.
3–4. winters' cold...summers' pride. Quarto has no genitive apostrophes here. One is clearly needed for 'summers', qualifying the noun *pride*; but *cold* too may be a noun, and 'winters' cold' would balance the second phrase. The plural verb (*Have*, l. 4) was often used with a singular subject. *10. his figure.* Its (i.e. beauty's) figure on the dial. *11. hue.* Complexion. *14. you.* The *age unbred*, l. 13.

33 (CVI).
1. the chronicle of wasted time. i.e. the medieval romances. *4. ladies dead and lovely knights.* The usual epithets would be 'lovely ladies and dead knights', but Shakespeare's thoughts are on the friend's masculine beauty. *5. blazon.* Literally, the description of a coat of arms in heraldry; here the listing of beautiful attributes. Cf. **1**.3. *9–10.* Like the prophecies of the Old Testament, held to prefigure the coming of Christ. *11. but...eyes.* With eyes that foresaw but could not physically see. *12. still.* As in Quarto, often emended to 'skill'. The sense is clear without changes; while lack of 'skill' seems to contradict ll. 5–8.

34 (CVII). A diversity of topical references has been claimed in *confined doom, mortal moon, eclipse, peace*; among dates proposed for the sonnet are: the Spanish Armada (1588), the Queen's 'grand climacteric' (1595), the rebellion of Essex (1601). All assume that *my true love* (l. 3), *my love* (l. 10), mean the friend in person. But if they allude to Shakespeare's love, its survival and renewal, the references may be just modifications of earlier sonnet images. Cf. *Idea* 12 and notes.
1. mine own fears. Concerning mutability or corruption of the friend's beauty or truth. *1–2. the prophetic soul...come.* Perhaps suggested by the 'prophecies' in 'the chronicle of wasted time' (**33**) whose ladies and knights were long since

dead. *3. lease.* Duration (on earth), as in *summer's lease,* **9**.4. *my true love.* The poet's love (see above). *4. forfeit...doom.* Completing the figure of *lease*; unlike other leases, love's cannot be forfeited by a limiting judgment. (For this sense of 'confined' and 'doom', cf. *Hamlet* I.v.10–11: '*Doom'd* for a certain term to walk the night, And for the day *confined* to fast in fires'.) *5.* The moon, though *mortal,* has *endured* eclipse; love too survives suspicion or jealousy. Contrast **17**.3. *6.* i.e. forebodings—by the poet, the friend, or others—of an end to friendship are now discredited. *7.* Uncertainties are personified as kings who, after a challenge to their succession, take the crown securely. As in l. 5, earlier images of negation are transcended; contrast **23**.5–8. *8.* Permanent peace of mind is an inference from the 'crowning' of *incertainties,* l. 7. Cf. *AS* 18.7: 'O, make in me those civil wars to cease'. *olives.* Symbolising peace and longevity, since these trees live to a great age. *10. My love.* The poet's affection, as in l. 3. *subscribes.* Gives priority (Latin, 'writes underneath'). *12. he insults.* Death triumphs. *dull and speechless tribes.* Unlettered barbarians, i.e. ordinary men without the poet's power to gain immortality. *13–14.* Paralleling **22**.1–8.

35 (CVIII).
1. character. Inscribe, represent. *2. true spirit.* Constancy. *3. new...now.* Changed to *new...new* by most editors since Malone. *5. prayers divine.* i.e. a set liturgy, as in the Book of Common Prayer. *8. hallowed thy fair name.* Suggested by the Lord's Prayer, 'hallowed be thy name'. *9. eternal love.* (Continues the parallels of divine service.) *love's fresh case.* The new circumstances of love; recalling *my love looks fresh,* **34**.10.

36 (CX).
2. a motley to the view. A patched coat in men's eyes; a figure for the public entertainer, like the fool in his motley, or for being 'all things to all men'. (It is most unlikely to mean that Shakespeare literally acted the fool's part.) *3. Gored mine own thoughts.* Open to various meanings: (1) 'put my thoughts in the stage fool's long coat' (*gore*); (2) 'inserted into my thoughts parti-coloured strips' (cf. *Twelfth Night* I.v.52: 'I wear not motley in my brain'); (3) 'let my thoughts be gored like a bear at the stake' (the usual but, in context, least likely interpretation). *4.* Turned new desires into habitual misconduct. *7. gave my heart another youth.* Made my love young again. *9. have.* Accept. *10–11.* 'I will make no new experiments with my feelings to test out my desire for an older friendship.' *13. next...best.* The best love, next to the love of heaven (in accord with the deification *A god in love,* l. 12).

37 (CXI).
1. with. For Quarto 'wish' (the medial 's' confused with 't'). *2. guilty goddess of.* Goddess guilty of (i.e. responsible for). *4. public means.* A livelihood dependent on the public. *public manners.* Common, undiscriminating behaviour. *6. subdued.* Subjected. *7. the dyer's hand.* (Stained by the material he works with.) *10. eisel.* Vinegar; associated with the *dyer's hand,* which was cleaned in vinegar; also drunk as a remedy against disease. *12. to correct correction.* To add punishment to punishment. *13. Pity me then.* 'But rather pity me'.

38 (CXV). Shakespeare's treatment of this theme may be compared with Donne's in *Love's Growth.*
5. reckoning Time. Taking into account what time could do.

Numbered by the million. *7. Tan.* Either darken, or coarsen (as skin turned into leather). *8. strong.* Constant. *10. then.* At that earlier time (alluded to in ll. 1-2). *11-12.* A variant of **34**.7; at that time, the 'crowning' of love was hastily performed, in fear of future events. *13. Love is a babe.* The ancient myth of Eros as a baby is absorbed into Shakespeare's own train of thought. *say so.* i.e. 'I could not love you dearer', l. 2. *14.* To treat the infant love as full-grown, though even now it is still growing.

39 (CXVI). Much of the power of this famous sonnet is gained by its telescoping of complex images or associations and re-statement of them in the simplest possible words.

1-2. 'Echoing the marriage service in the Book of Common Prayer: "If any of you know cause, or just impediment, why these two persons should not be joined together in holy matrimony, ye are to declare it". The "impediments" not admitted are change of circumstances (l. 3) and inconstancy (l. 4)' (Dover Wilson). *4. bends.* Changes course. *with the remover to remove.* To absent itself when the other's love is absent. *5. mark.* Sea-mark or lighthouse, in contrast to the waves as an image of time (**23**.1-4). *7.* The traditional image of love as a storm-tossed ship (cf. Wyatt 2, *Amor.* 14) is replaced by love as the guiding star. *8.* Navigators took the height of the north star to guide their course; so love directs man's course in life, though its essential nature, like the star's, is unknown. *9. Time's fool.* The dupe of time and change; cf. 'thought's the slave of life, and life, time's fool', *I Henry IV*, v.iv.81. *9-10. rosy lips and cheeks Within his bending sickle's compass come.* Couples the image of the rose with that of time's scythe, as in **23**.9-12. *11. his.* i.e. Time's. *12. doom.* The Last Judgment, as in **22**.13. *13-14.* 'If this view of love be a fallacy, and proved so in my case, there was never such thing as man's love, and hence my verse could never have been written.'

40 (CXIX).

1. siren tears. False sympathy. Cf. Lodge's *Rosalynde:* 'In choice of friends, beware of light belief...The Siren's tears do threaten mickle grief' (ed. Greg, p. 7). In classical lore, sirens were women who lured men with their tears; but in medieval bestiaries they became poisonous serpents; hence the *potions* (l. 1) and *limbecks* (alembics) (l. 2). *2. within.* In their true nature. *7. spheres.* Eyesockets. *fitted.* Shaken by a fit. *8. madding.* Driving to madness. *14. ills.* As in Quarto; sometimes emended to 'ill', but ll. 1-8 refer to more than one evil.

41 (CXX). The poet's desertion of the friend is equated in terms of suffering to the friend's rejection of the poet, and the 'humble salve' of remorse, offered once by the friend (**16**), is reciprocated.

3. under...bow. 'Show contrition for my own wrongdoing.' *4. nerves.* Usually explained as 'strength' (the earlier meaning), but the modern use, 'sensibilities', seems to be included. Cf. *my deepest sense*, l. 10. *7. a tyrant.* In arbitrary or ill-considered behaviour. *9. remembered.* Reminded. *13-14.* The friend's wrongdoing provides a fund of moral credit on which the poet may draw; each can now ransom the other from guilt.

42 (CXXIII). Takes up the affirmations of constancy in **39**. Another sonnet providing doubtful evidence for dating.

2-4. Hotson (*Shakespeare's Sonnets Dated*) takes this as a reference to the obelisks of Celsus, exacavated and re-erected in Rome 1585-90, and dates the sonnets within those years. But mention could have been made considerably later; besides, *pyramids* was more probably suggested by Horace's *pyramidum altius* (see note to **22**.1–8). As 'Time's pyramids', the reference is not to man-made structures, but rather to nature's mountain-peaks. Among Ovid's examples of eternal recurrence (see note to **24**.5–8) was the evidence of anchors and sea-shells proving that mountain tops were once under the sea, while mountains in turn were brought down to sea level. *5–8.* 'We marvel at seeming novelties because our lives are too short to remember when they existed before; new inventions are really an old story.' *6. foist.* Offer as if new. *7. born...desire.* Born according to our wish (cf. Ovid: *nascique vocatur | incipere esse aliud, quam quod fuit ante*—'being born only means beginning to be different from what was before'. *12.* (Linking past and present events to ever-changing growth and decline.)

43 (CXXIV). The image of love as a growing child develops from 'Love is a babe', **38**.13–14, and is fused with earlier images of flowers, monuments, and kings to suggest now a transcendence of 'state', i.e. fortune and time.
1. my dear love. The poet's love, not a term for the friend (cf. 'my true love', **34**.3). *child of state.* Offspring of circumstances. *2.* Love might lose its rightful 'father' (the poet) and be treated as a mere by-blow of fortune or chance. *3.* Recalling 'Love's not Time's fool', **39**.9. *4.* Reaped by Time, with other weeds or flowers; cf. 'rosy lips and cheeks', **39**.9. *5.* Re-states the image of love as a restored building in **40**.11–12 in contrast to the mutability of 'gilded monuments' (**22**.1) *6–7.* The 'child of state' metaphor blends into the recurrent image of a monarch threatened by rebels (**23**.6–7, **34**.7–8, **38**.12). *thralled.* Oppressed. *8.* 'To which the inducements of the time call people like us (*our fashion*).' Discontent—political, social, and religious—was rife at the turn of the century and came to a head in Essex's rebellion (1601) which implicated Southampton. *9. Policy, that heretic.* Suggested by 'state', l. 1. *Policy*, i.e. political opportunism, was inherently amoral, hence a *heretic*. Linked with Fortune and Time it 'plotted' against Love. *10. Leases...hours.* Cf. **34**.3–4. *11.* Love is thus not a *child of state*, nor a victim of *Policy*, but a great independent republic. *12.* (Unlike the weeds and flowers of l. 9.) *13. fools of time.* Victims of history or politics. *14.* 'Who die for high principles, having lived for evil (*crime*)'. This may be a specific reference, possibly to Essex, or to Catholic plotters; but if so it has been carefully veiled.

44 (CXXVI). Not a formal sonnet, but an *envoi* in couplets, completing either all the collection of sonnets to the friend, or a series. It has been suggested that the poem accompanied the gift of an hour-glass.
2. Time is an hour-glass, from which beauty pours out like sand, the com-pleted hour serving, like Time's sickle, to destroy it. By holding the glass, the 'lovely boy' has Time in his power. *3. by waning grown.* The friend is also the hour-glass itself, and not subject to it: as his 'sand' is *waning* in the upper receptacle, it has *grown* in the lower one; being Time's master, his beauty is enhanced as his years run out. *3–4. and therein...grow'st.* Cut by Time's sickle, the 'lovers' wither, while the friend continues to grow. *5. wrack.* Destruction. *8. Time disgrace.* Shame Time's power. *9. minion.* Darling, favourite. *11. Her audit.* Nature's account to Time. *12.* 'Her quittance as having rendered a true

account is obtained by surrendering you.' From *quietus est*, the formal approbation of the steward's account.)

All the following sonnets are addressed to a dark-haired, black-eyed mistress, whose looks challenge the convention of blonde beauty as her conduct violates the convention of chastity. See Introd., pp. 21–2.

45 (CXXVII).
1. fair. With play on 'blonde' and 'beautiful'. *2*. 'Or if in fact beautiful, it was not called so.' *3. Beauty's successive heir*. Rightful successor to the title of beauty, with a pun on *heir* and 'hair'. *4. a bastard shame*. A rival *heir* (hair) who disgraces Beauty by claiming to be her child (referring to wigs or hair-dyes, ll. 5–6). *5*. i.e. every woman has taken over Nature's power to decide the colour of her hair. *6. Fairing the foul*. Turning dark into fair, ugliness into beauty. *Art's*. Artifice's. *9. raven*. (1) black; (2) ill-boding. *10. Her eyes so suited*. 'Eyes' seems repetitive, hence some editors change it to 'brow(s)'; but this is unwarranted by the context. *suited*. Dressed in black (hence like *mourners*). *as*. Dover Wilson's emendation of Quarto 'and' (less drastic than reading *eyes* as 'brows'). *12. creation*. What was intended at their creation. *esteem*. Reputation. *13. so...becoming*. So becomingly they mourn.

46 (CXXVIII).
2. that blessed wood. The keys of the virginals, not plated with ivory like harpsichords and modern pianos. *3. sway'st*. Governest. *5. those jacks*. Wooden uprights which struck the strings when the keys were pressed; in testing, they might be held down with the palm of the hand. Also with word-play on 'jacks' as a contemptuous word for 'men'. *8. stand*. Do not move. *10. chips*. Keys.

47 (CXXIX). The momentum of this invective against lust over-rides quatrain units, metrical norms and sentence divisions, only halting at l. 12. Action, anticipation and retrospect are telescoped in the vision of emotional chaos;
1. expense of spirit. (1) Spiritual exhaustion; (2) squandering of sperm. *waste*. Probably with word-play on 'waist'. *4. to trust*. To be trusted. *10. in quest to have, extreme*. Quarto prints 'in quest, to haue extreame': with the shift of comma, the future objective complements past *Had*, present *having*. *11. in proof*. To be tried out. *proved, a very*. Quarto 'proud and very'. *14*. Compare Lodge's 'A heaven in show, a hell to them that prove' (*Rosalynde*, 1590.)

48 (CXXX). The satire is not on the mistress, but on the conventional eulogies of minor sonnets in vogue from about 1592. It ends with a qualified but acceptable compliment.
1–2. Cf. Lodge's *Phyllis* (1593) VIII: 'No stars her eyes to clear the wandering night, / But shining suns of true divinity /...No coral is her lip.../ But even that crimson that adorns the sun.' *4. wires*. Usually suggesting fine-spun gold. *5. damasked*. Refers to the 'variegated damask', which bore white and pink flowers on the same tree. *8. reeks*. Is exhaled. (The word did not mean 'to smell repulsively' until the late seventeenth century.) *11–12*. Contrast Lodge, *Phyllis* VIII: 'No nymph is she, but mistress of the air.' *go*. Walk. *13–14. as rare As any she*. 'As unusual—or remarkable—as any other woman.' *14. belied*. Who is belied.

49 (CXXXIII). The situation parallels that of **19**, and perhaps of **15–17**.

1. that heart. The mistress's. *5-6. Me...my self...my next self.* She has not only taken his own heart from him, but his friend's. *engrossed.* monopolised. *9-10.* The conceit is of two hearts imprisoned in the mistress's bosom. He allows his own heart to be placed in her *steel bosom's ward*, but asks for it in turn to confine (*bail*) his friend's. His own heart will thus be the 'prison' (*guard*), and she will not be able to ill-treat the 'prisoner' in the poet's gaol.

50 (CXXXVII). On the confusion of eyes and heart, perception and cognition.

1. Thou blind fool Love. This is Shakespeare's only reference in the *Sonnets* to the traditional image of Blind Eros or Cupid. *2. see not what they see.* Do not see the reality. *4.* Yet take the worst for the best. *5-8.* The emotional dilemma is reflected in the random associations *bay—ride—hooks—tied. 5. over-partial.* Excessively biased. *6. the bay where all men ride.* The sea as an unconscious female symbol suggests the conscious sexual pun *ride* and leads to the images of ll. 7-8. *7-8.* Judgment, the heart's function, is caught like a fish by the falsehood of eyes to which the heart is tied. *9-10. several plot...common place.* Private ground... open common. Cf. *Caelica* 1.13-14. *14. this false plague.* The plague of falsehood.

51 (CXXXVIII).

3. untutored. Untrained, inexperienced. *5. vainly.* In self-deception. *7. Simply.* Pretending to be simple (as against authentic *simple truth*, l. 8). *9. unjust.* Unfaithful. *11. habit.* Demeanour. *12. age in love.* 'an old person in love', or 'age, in matters of love'. *told.* (1) Counted; (2) talked of. *13.* (One *lies*, and is thus lain with: falsehood and the act of love, described by the same word, become synonymous.) *14. flattered.* Gratified.

52 (CXLIV). Allusions to *better angel, side, hell,* are sometimes understood as equivocations on sexual organs, intercourse, venereal disease, etc. Shakespeare was quite capable of such innuendoes, but the intensity of tone, and grim angel-fiend polarity, makes them unlikely in this context of spiritual crisis.

1. (The friend and the mistress.) *2. suggest me still.* Constantly prompt me to action (like the good and bad spirits in *Doctor Faustus*). The concept of 'twin loves', a *bonus daemon* (good spirit) seeking to elevate the soul, and a *malus daemon* (bad spirit) seeking to degrade it to hell, belongs to the Renaissance Platonism of Ficino. *4. coloured ill.* (As in **45**). *5-6.* Cf. *Othello* v.ii.210-11: 'This sight would make him do a desperate turn, Yea, curse his better angel from his side'. *side.* Quarto has 'sight', an obvious non-rhyming slip; *side* is in the earlier version of this sonnet, printed in *The Passionate Pilgrim* (1599). (According to the 'priapic' interpretation, *hell*=vagina, *better angel*=penis, *side*=trunk of the body.) *8. foul.* So Quarto; *Passionate Pilgrim* has 'faire'. *Pride.* Lust. *9.* i.e. whether the friend has been corrupted. *12. one angel in another's hell.* The good angel (friend) may be in the bad angel's (the Mistress's) hell. *14. fire my good one out.* Drives my friend (the 'good angel') out. (Sometimes argued to be an equivocation on *fire*, 'gives venereal disease'.)

53 (CXLVI). The body-soul polarity here works on a different level from the eyes-heart contrasts of **50**, based on secular psychology. As **47** recalls Sidney's 'Thou blind man's mark', so this sonnet resembles his 'Leave me, O love', and has affinities with sonnets of meditation by Donne and others.

1. sinful earth. The body with its humours and appetites, 'concupiscible' and 'irascible'. *2. Foiled by.* Quarto has 'My sinful earth', which is repetitive, and metrically wrong. Some verb has been lost which takes up the images of siege (*rebel powers, array*) and *array* as adornment. *Foiled* could mean (1) frustrated; (2) outwardly adorned or gilded; the first sense is taken up in l. 3, the second in l. 4. *5–6. so short a lease...thy fading mansion.* Recurrent images of life's brevity, as in **19**, **43** and elsewhere. *8. thy charge.* What you have paid dearly for. *9. thy servant's.* i.e. the body's. *10. aggravate.* increase. *thy store.* The soul's, as against the body's store which 'pines'. *11. terms divine.* Periods of time by divine reckonings ('a thousand years in thy sight are considered as a day'). *13.* Death, identified with worms that feed on the body, will itself be fed on by the soul. Cf. Donne, *HS* 6.14.

54 (CXLVII).
1. as a fever. Cf. 'this false plague', **50**.14. *2.* Referring to the thirst whose quenching was thought to aggravate fever. *4. appetite.* Either the sick man's fancies or sexual desire. *7. approve.* Confirm from experience. *8. which...except.* Which (i.e. *desire*) medical advice objected to. *9.* The proverb went 'past cure, past care'; here it is inverted. Being past the care of the 'physician' reason, the poet is 'past cure'. *14. as black as hell.* Renounces the sophistries of **45**, and implicitly confirms the serious, non-quibbling use of 'hell' in **52**.5 ('To win me soon to hell') and **52**.12 ('one angel in another's hell').

FULKE GREVILLE, LORD BROOKE

The text is based on Bullough's edition. Most of Greville's writings were unpublished at his death. *Caelica*, which appeared in 1633, was probably written over the 1590s and early 1600s. For general comments see Introd., pp. 24–6.

1 (XXXVIII). Paradise and the Fall supply a dream image of the lover's desires and self-frustration. The symbolism has curious resemblances to Blake's in *The Garden of Love*.
1. overnight. (In dreams). *finely used.* handsomely treated. *3. refused.* Denied. *4. part.* A share (of enjoyment). *5. curious Knowledge.* (1) his own inquisitive rationality, personified as an enemy to his sensuous joys; (2) the Tree of Knowledge in Eden, which here conceals fruits instead of offering them. *busy flame.* Officious zeal. *7. for.* Because. *9. Rumour.* Report. *11. glassy.* Both fragile and mirror-like, since through it the poet becomes conscious of his own shortcomings. *Tender of.* Attendant to. *12. Seraphin.* Like a Seraph (with Hebrew plural suffix *-im*, or *-in*, taken as part of the name). In Gen. iii.24 the guardians of Eden were called Cherubim, another order of angels; but the Seraphim, creatures of fire, were associated with love in Christian interpretations. *13–14.* The paradise of love, from which the poet is driven, turns out to be (*is proved*) common ground available to all. (Cf. *ShS* 50.9–10.)

2 (XXXIX). The Tower of Babel provides a conceit reinforcing the conclusion of **1**. Typically of 'metaphysical' verse, the image has an intellectual relevance but no sensuous resemblance to the experience of courtship.
1. flesh. Man's depraved nature. *reach.* Contrivance. *2. overreach.* Overpower. *3.* The biblical account of the Flood (Gen. vi–viii) precedes that of the Tower (Gen. xi). *for it.* For the 'pride of flesh'. *4. Babylon.* Babel (the Hebraic form). *not to die.* Without being punished by death (in accordance with God's promise,

Gen. viii.21). *6.* Who wished to overcome heaven's will (*destiny*) with cunning device (*policy*). *8. speak.* Rhyming with *break*, l. 6. *10. seat.* Site. *11. myself... intend.* Directed my course there (to Caelica's heart, identified with Babylon). *12. natural kindness...passion's art.* Affection is associated with nature; passion, in the sense of 'passionate speech', with art. *13. free.* Admitted to privileges.

3 (LXXXV). 'The poem...is one of the triumphs of the plain style' (Gunn). Love has the Christian-Platonic meaning of a physical experience that shadows forth spiritual perfection.

2. Done and begun. The reversal of normal sequence suggests not only the practice of sexual love, but the ending of physical experience by death, which commences a new mode of love in the afterlife. *3. first and last.* Love, as a manifestation of the divine, inheres in life from beginning to end. 'I am Alpha and Omega, the beginning and the ending' (Rev. i.8). *4. End.* As both culmination and objective. *alone.* In and for itself. 'Our love for God is both a way to the absolute, and—being an image or imitation of God's love—is in another sense already of the absolute, the end itself' (Gunn). *7. refined.* Purified. *10.* An unchangeable essence underlying the *passions* (perturbations of the mind) which are *overthrown.* *11. objects.* Objectives. *13. frame.* 'Form, attribute, or emanation' (Bullough). *14. by...else.* When attributed to all other qualities (except eternity).

4 (C). A reflection based on the familiar romance theme of the lover's thoughts at night. Darkness may be an image of hell, or hell a projection of the imagination in darkness.

2. Direction may have been subjectively *lost*, or, as a property of light, have *gone down.* *5. vain.* Pointless. *the inward sense.* Sensibilities that function without physical perception. *6. witty tyranny.* Tyranny of the mind (unchecked by reality) *7. thorough self-offence.* Through injury done to itself (referring to the mind rather than its fear). *9. depriving darknesses.* The darkness of the soul depriving man of true vision; with implications of hell's darkness. *10. reflections...error.* Projections of moral error. *12. hurt imaginations.* Taking up the 'self-offence' of the mind, l. 7.

5 (CII).
1. probability. Knowledge based on rational proof. 'Greville means the sphere of metaphysical enquiry in which human reason tries to solve the eternal problems' (Bullough). *3. Opinion.* Self-conceit personified. *see,.* The comma has been added, since the nouns in l. 4 are best understood in apposition to *probability*, not as objects of *see.* *4. party.* Part or member of truth, regarded as a body. (Greville hesitates between seeing 'probability' as an *enemy of truth* (l. 2) and as its weak limb.) *barrenness.* (Bringing forth no vital truth.) *6. obedience.* i.e. to God. *wit.* Intellect. *8.* Reason fashions God in the form of man's flesh (instead of man made in the image of God). *9. The word of power.* 'In the beginning was the Word...and the Word was God...All things were made by him' (John i.1–3). *10.* Till the Second Coming and the Resurrection. *the veils be rent.* As reported after the Crucifixion: 'And behold, the veil of the temple was rent in twain' (Matt. xxviii.51, also Mark and Luke). *14. wrap up.* Involve or enfold so as to obscure or disguise.

SIR WILLIAM DRUMMOND OF HAWTHORNDEN

Drummond's *Poems*, including a series in the second part entitled *Urania, or Spiritual Poems*, appeared in 1616. They were followed by *Flowers of Zion* (1630). The present text is based upon Kastner's edition.

1 (*Poems* 1, v). The '*How...If...*' structure recalls *AS* 14, but Drummond's speculations are about cosmic, not political questions. The love statement in the couplet is conventional and perfunctory.
   1. entitled First. The first of the nine concentric spheres or 'heavens' in Ptolemy's system was that of the moon, beneath which all things were changing and mortal. *2. worlds.* Planets or heavenly bodies seen as inhabited. *3.* (Such people, living above the moon's sphere, would presumably be immortal.) *4. essence pure.* Made of spiritual substance. *5. fixed...gold.* The 'fixed stars', so called because their positions in the sky did not vary. *6. wandering carbuncles.* Planets, which change position, compared to reddish jewels. *7-8.* (Set in rotating spheres, the stars were thought to be propelled in an opposite direction by some material or spiritual force.) *9. posts.* Travels with speed. *night's pale queen.* (From *Delia* 9.6) *10. borrowed.* (From the sun.) *11. Iris.* The rainbow, associated with the Greek goddess Iris, a messenger of the gods. *13-14.* Cf. *AS* 14.13-14. *eye...thee.* Near-rhymes in Scots pronunciation.

2 (*Poems* 1, vii). On the idea of the soul's pre-existence, propounded by Plato in *Phaedo*.
   1. The learned Grecian. Cf. *AS* xxv.1: 'The wisest scholar of the wight most wise.' *2. passing sense.* Surpassing human faculties. *8. toiled.* Wearied. *to...rebel.* That militates against reason (such as sensual desires, contrasted to the spiritual love of pre-existence). *9. Most true it is.* Echoing *AS* 4.1-2, but without Sidney's irony. *11. Idea.* In the Platonic sense, the ideal beauty of which earthly beauty is a mere reflection, and based on the Platonic theory of thought as recollection.

3 (*Poems* 1, viii). Freely rendered from Petrarch's sonnet '*Or, che 'l cielo e la terra e 'l vento tace*', also imitated by Surrey.
   2. coach. The coach of night (Petrarch's *carro stellato*, 'starry chariot'), corresponding to the chariot of the sun-god which was given across the sky by day. *3. Tethys' azure bed.* The ocean; Tethys in Greek mythology was the wife of Okeanos, and bore the nymphs Okeanids (l. 4). *4.* Drummond associates Tethys' sea-nymphs with the celestial nymphs, companions of the moon-goddess. *the Pole.* A fixed point in the sky about which the stars were thought to revolve. *5. Cynthia.* The moon as a goddess. *cypress.* Light, transparent fabric, originally from Cyprus. *6. The Latmian shepherd.* Endymion, the young shepherd who slept in a cave on Mount Latmos, where he was visited by the enamoured moon. *7-8. whiles...Whiles.* Now...Now (a Scots form). *11. Proteus' monstrous people.* The seals (and by extension, sea-monsters) tended by the Greek demi-god Proteus.

4 (*Poems* 1, ix). Suggested by *AS* 18, but with no explicit mention of love.
   3. Cf. Sidney's 'The indifferent judge between the high and low'. *8. spares.* Variant of 'sparest', in the interest of the metre. *14.* Sleep was traditionally called the image of death. The 'kiss of death' was a term of Renaissance

Platonists for the union of the soul with Christ. Drummond's variation on Sidney's ending is significant.

5 (*Poems* II (unnumbered; Kastner, ii, p. 82). Entitled 'Tears on the Death of Moeliades' (anagram of *miles a deo*, 'soldier sent from God'). A lament on the death of Prince Henry, James I's eldest son, in 1612 at the age of 18.

1. glance. Flash or gleam. *3. of contraries.* See note to Donne, *HS* 15.1. *7–8.* (The Parthian shaft was an arrow shot backwards; from the practice of the mounted Parthian archers in Roman times.) Drummond's image suggests the action of death, destroying men as they pursue life. *12. Thrall.* Enslave. *14.* (Implying, as throughout the sonnet, that death is an inherent part of life.)

6 (*Urania* i). On the Ovidian theme of universal mutability, but resolved on a Christian note. The opening suggests sonnets of Castiglione, Du Bellay, and Spenser lamenting the ruins of Rome, but Drummond's references are more general.

1. crowns of bays. Wreaths of bay-leaves, worn by Roman conquerors. *3. lays.* Songs. *5.* Unlike most previous treatments, this sonnet points out the slaughter that accompanies ambition. *6.* From far north to far south; based on Seneca's use of evocative names to suggest great reaches of space. *Tanais:* Classical name for a river in Scythia, now the Don. *7. frames.* Structures or political systems. *held.* Considered (to be). *8. sport of days.* Plaything of time. *9–12.* Repeats Ovid, *Metamorphoses* xv, on mutability (cf. *ShS* 25). But *beneath the moon* (l. 12) implies that only sublunary things change; hence the exhortation of the couplet. *14. unkown to nature.* (Pertaining to spiritual experience.)

7 (*Flowers of Zion* xix). Entitled 'Earth and all on it Changeable'. The Ovidian theme of the interchange of land and sea (cf. *ShS* 24) stimulated antiquarian and geological enquiries in Drummond's time.

1. that space. Where the English Channel is situated. *4. dear.* Strenuous, difficult. *tile.* A variant of either 'toil' (Kastner) or 'till' (suggested Bullough), in Scots making a near-rhyme with *isle*, l. 2. *5–8.* Stating the converse of ll. 1–4; today's cultivated land and great cities were once marshes or under the sea. *6. shires enwalled.* Suggested by Sylvester's translation of Du Bartas' praise of France: 'thy Cities, shires do seem'. *7. marish.* Marsh. *8. Proteus' flocks.* See note to **3**.11. *11. turn.* Return. *12.* Cf. *Delia* 4.1. *13–14. that lies...prized.* Echoing *Delia* 4.4.

8 (*Flowers of Zion* xxii). Entitled 'The Praise of Solitary Life'.

2. his own. To himself, not dependent on others. *3.* 'Who, though choosing solitude, is not left alone'. *6. the widowed dove.* A traditional example, and here, reminder, of constancy in love. *8.* 'Which make good counsel seem doubtful, and approve evil.' *9. Zephyr('s).* Greek personification of the west wind: a soft, gentle breeze. *12. to poison...gold.* In contrast to evil absorbed in wealth and state. *14.* Resembling Sidney's poem in the *Arcadia:* 'Sweet woods, the delight of solitariness'.

9 (*Flowers of Zion* xxiii). Entitled 'To a Nightingale'. Traditionally the nightingale's song expressed love or desire. But Drummond's song 'void of care' rather anticipates Keats's ode.

2. Without care of either winters past or those to come. *8. A...sense.* Shaming the human attitude or response. *lowers.* Degrades itself. *10. Attired.* Adorned.

11. Quite. Completely. *spites.* Acts of malice. *13. Song-star.* 'Songstarre' in the 1630 edn., punning in Scots on 'songster'. *14. Airs of spheres.* Music of the spheres; the spiritual harmonies believed to result from the turning upon one another of the celestial spheres.

10 (*Flowers of Zion* xxiv). Entitled 'Content and Resolute'. Modelled on Guglia's sonnet *'Come s'avien che città degna e pura'* ('As when it happens that a city worthy and pure') (1586).

5. thralls. Captives. *6. spite.* Outrage, injury. *7. fane.* ('Phan', edn. 1630). Temple or holy place. *9. wrack.* Wreck. ('Wrake', edn. 1630, an eye-rhyme with *make*, l. 12.) *13–14.* Based on *ShS* 13.13–14. Guglia concludes by speaking of the heart: *Che vivra, spero, eterno al caldo, al gielo | Malgrado al mondo, a morte, al tempo avaro.* '(Which will live, I hope, eternal in heat and frost, despite the world, and death, and avaricious time'.)

WILLIAM ALABASTER

1–2 are from *Personal Sonnets,* **3–10** from *Divine Meditations,* in Story and Gardner's edition (1959), from which the numbers in brackets are taken.

1 (XLVII). Cf. Sidney's reference to well-wishing friends in *AS* 11.

1. My friends. Colleagues at Cambridge; also near relatives (commonly termed 'friends'). Alabaster's uncle, his old schoolmaster, and the Master of Trinity College, pointed out the distress his decision to become a Catholic was causing. *2. run.* Act without restraint. *4. You feel...we find.* 'You suffer directly, we experience the mental grief.' *6. bill.* Inventory (of benefits forfeited and ills to accrue). *8. behind.* Still to be listed. *9. transel'mented to steel.* Changed from the elements or substance (of flesh) to that of steel. Cf. 'my steeled sense' in *ShS* cxII.8. *10. this...that...all.* Objects of *feel,* whose subject is *sense,* l. 9. *12. Not so, nor so.* Cf. *AS* 29.12–13: ' "What, is it thus?" Fie, no. / "Or so?" Much less'. *13–14.* Echoing in a devotional context Sidney's acceptance of the consequences of love in *AS* 9.13–14.

2 (XLVIII).

1. myself. 'My own former personality'. *2. state.* Way of life. *strength.* Resources. *3. unprovoked...disease.* Pleasant restlessness felt in the voluntary (*unprovoked*) pursuit of studies. *4. nature and engrafted kind.* Natural traits and those planted by nurture or training. *5. cleaving twist.* Rope or strand of close attachment. *distant tempers.* Inclinations leading far (from these). (He has renounced the characteristics of his nature and upbringing which hold back straying inclinations.) *6–7.* The courteous, sensitive approach that esteems (*doth praise*) other persons' grave opinions in order to please them. *11. transelement.* See note to **1.**9. *14.* That the desire for love may cause him to be possessed by love, and the possession augment his desire.

3 (I). An introduction to the meditations which follow.

1. night. The darkness that fell after the Crucifixion: 'Now from the sixth hour there was darkness over all the land unto the ninth hour' (Matt. xxvii.45; also Mark and Luke). Story and Gardner see here an allusion to the night of the Last Supper: 'when they had sung an hymn, they went out into the Mount of Olives' (Matt. xxvi. 30, etc.). *passion.* Suffering, specifically that of Jesus on the cross. *2. heaven beneath.* (Since Jesus was divine, heaven was his ambience on earth.) *3. sound the onset.* Signal the attack (the harrying of hell). *4. foes.* (The literal meaning of 'fiends'.) *7. Surcharged.* Overwhelmed. *thrall.* Distress. *10. the portrait…me.* Adapted from the Petrarchan conceit of the portrait of the mistress in the lover's heart; cf. Donne, *HS* 9.2–3. *14.* May not decline to grant (*refuse*) fire to the coldest ice (used figuratively for those lacking zeal; in **10**.8, for the poet's own heart).

4 (III). The text on which he meditates serves to expose the instability of his faith as a man.

1. Over…Cedron. 'He went forth with his disciples over the brook of Cedron, where was a garden' (John xviii.1, indicating the place where Jesus was arrested and taken for trial; in other gospel accounts the garden was named Gethsemane and located in or near the Mount of Olives). *2. entertain.* Take upon himself. *3–4.* Christian exegesis, which interpreted Old Testament events as prefiguring the gospel, identified Cedron with the 'brook of water' crossed by King David in his flight from the rebellious Absalom (II Sam. xvii.20–2). This is named in verse 22 as the Jordan, whereas the Mount of Olives rises above Jerusalem. *5. passion.* As in **3**.1, but here applied to the agony in Gethsemane (Luke xxii.44). *6.* The brook becomes an allegorical symbol of the world. *walloweth.* Surges. *8. resolution.* Confidence, conviction. *9. he… clear.* He must have passed completely. *12. unfaithful.* Not to be trusted.

5 (X). The process of meditation is inverted: confident assertions of faith in the octave are 'placed' in the sestet as the thoughts of one whose faith failed him.

2–4. Plays on *will* as (1) desire; (2) mental power; (3) consent. Having chained his desire to Christ's will, he has no power to unbind it again, but will stay with full consent. *6.* Cf. **3**.10 and note. *9.* Matt. xxvi.35: 'Peter said unto him, Though I should die with thee, yet will I not deny thee'; Mark xiv.29: 'But Peter said unto him, "Although all shall be offended, yet will not I".' Peter's 'denials', dissociating himself from Jesus, are recounted later in the same chapters. *10. swell.* Be filled with pride (cf. Donne, *HS* 6.12). *13–14. what might…so.* By what action he might learn to pledge his faith truly through hearing the reciprocal pledge made by Christ.

6 (XXIII).

1. from…mire. From the depths of hell, into which Jesus descended before rising at Easter (cf. 'this miry flood', **4**.11.) *6. close.* Enclose. *9–14.* The unusual rhyme-scheme of the sestet may have been influenced by the French form, which has a couplet at ll. 9–10, followed by a Petrarchan quatrain. *9–10.* Hell finds its subjective correspondence in the poet's heart, where Christ instead of rising has been poisoned by the Devil and lies dead. (Cf. Donne's 'Reason, your viceroy', *HS* 10.7–8. *14. a dreadful argument.* A theme to be considered with dread.

7 (XXVI). The conceit sees unfallen man as 'like cedars'; men after the Fall as the thorns of which Christ's crown was made; and men redeemed by Christ as thorns transformed into roses.

1. delicious. Affording pleasure (the meaning of the Hebrew 'Eden'). *2. like cedars.* 'The righteous…shall grow like a cedar in Lebanon' (Psalm xcii.12). *4–5.* Suggested by the curse laid on Adam: 'Thorns also and thistles shall it [the tree of knowledge] bring forth to thee' (Gen. iii.18). Identified with men after the Fall, the thorns become armed rebels against heaven, like the Titans of Greek mythology (cf. Gen. vi.4: 'There were giants in the earth in those days'). *6. coronal.* Circlet for the head (the crown of thorns worn by Jesus at the Crucifixion). *8. crown* (2). For 'crowned' in Mss., which probably came from a misreading of Alabaster's original spelling 'crowne' as 'crownd'; 'd' and 'e' being almost indistinguishable in Elizabethan secretary hand. *9. tincture.* Dye. *12. odorant strain.* Stock that will be able to emit fragrance. Story and Gardner take from one Ms. 'odious strain', and alter this to 'odious stain'. *14.* That the virtues of redeemed man should henceforth crown Christ with roses.

8 (XXXVIII). On the mystery of eternity and time, with its personal significance. *1.* Stating the metaphysical paradox of creation in eternity. *2.* Develops the paradox: duration is attached to endlessness like thread wound round a ball (*bottom*). *3-4.* Any point of the thread of duration shows eternity half in the past and half yet to come, though there is neither beginning nor end. *5. conjoined, both unseparated.* Duration as a combining of the threads of past and future, though no distinction between them exists in eternity. *6. dated is by motion.* Time as an aspect of duration is *dated* or marked off by virtue of movement. *7. everness actuated.* Eternity given the property of action. *9. clew.* Synonymous with 'bottom', l. 2. *10. overfathom.* Understand and transcend. (A word seemingly coined by Alabaster.) *12. that unbounded clime.* Eternity expressed in space rather than time, as a region (*clime*) without boundaries. *13. designs.* Intentions. *14. under compass.* Within the limits. *level.* Aim (like a gun).

9 (LXIII). *1-2. The first beginning...Was God.* 'In the beginning God created the heaven and the earth' (Gen. i.1). *2. end.* (1) Last act of creation; (2) final cause, as against God, the 'first cause'; (3) end or purpose (of creation). *3.* (In Christ, as God and man.) *4. one person.* As a Person of the Trinity. *5. nature's circle.* The completed cycle of nature, from God's creation of the universe to his manifestation in man. *6. pale.* Boundary. *circulet.* Circlet. (Christ is identified with *nature's circle*, l. 5, and *the Godhead's ring*, l. 8.) *9. two rings.* Divinity and nature in the created world. *one diamond.* Jesus in his life on earth. (The double ring fastened by a jewel was a fashionable style.) *11.* Natural creatures in their multiplicity, God in his unity. *more and one.* The One and the many are united there. *12. Alpha and Omega.* First and last letters of the Greek alphabet. 'I am Alpha and Omega, the beginning and the ending' (Rev. i.8). *tablet.* slab of stone, metal etc. bearing an inscription. *13-14. the angels' alphabet, Jesus.* With play on *alphabet* as the key to or rudiments of study (OED 2). The conceit is based on the child's 'hornbook': a leaf of paper with the alphabet and numbers, covered by transparent horn and mounted on a tablet (suggested by Bullough).

10 (LXXIII). In contrast to Christ, in whom the divine and the human coincide (**9**), the poet as a man suffers from the contradiction between his heavenly reason and his earthly heart. Cf. *HS* 15.
2. move and rest. The verbs relate respectively to *heaven* and *earth*: in the Ptolemaic universe the heavens rotate while the earth is stationary. *3-4.* Man as the microcosm of the universe combines a mobile, heavenly mind with a static, 'dead' heart. *5. circulize.* Make to rotate. *8. this ice.* The heart seen as a glacial region. *9-11.* The orbit of reason as 'sun' is described through the seasons of winter when it moves south, *equinoctial* spring and autumn, and summer when it rises *higher* (more northerly). *10. both.* The heavenly poles of day and

night. *12*. In all the seasons of *thoughts' unrest* (l. 6), the heart's sea remains
frozen over. *13. the Son*. With wordplay on Christ as the divine Sun, who can
melt the 'sea glacial' of the heart. *14*. Echoing the Lord's prayer: 'Thy will be
done in earth, as it is in heaven' (Matt. vi.10).

JOHN DONNE

The order follows Helen Gardner's edition of the *Divine Poems* (1952, 1959)
Sonnets **1–6** were probably completed in the first half of 1609, **7–10** a few
months later. The first set is broadly a meditation on the 'Four Last Things';
the others are further meditations on God's love for man (**7–9**) and man's
love for God (**10**). But the structure is much affected by emotional tensions,
rebellious questionings, and oscillations of mood. See Introd., pp. 28–30. **11–12**
are two of four penitential sonnets written before 1610.

    1. 'A preparatory prayer before making a meditation' (Gardner).
    1. titles. Martz (1) cites Puente's Jesuit colloquy urging men in meditation to
offer to God 'titles and reasons...to grant us what we demand'. But Donne
refers to *God's* 'titles' (i.e. claims), not man's. *3. decayed*. Ruined (by man's
first sin). *5*. Cf. Matt. xiii.43: 'Then shall the righteous shine forth as the sun
in the kingdom of their father'. The 'son-sun' wordplay is already latent in the
translated text. *6*. Alludes to the parable of the labourers in the vineyard,
Matt. xx.1–16. *7–8. sheep...image...temple*. Biblical images; from Matt. xviii.
12–14, where man, the stray sheep, is found by the Shepherd; Gen. i.27: 'So
God created man in his own image'; I Cor. vi.19: 'Your body is the temple
of the Holy Ghost.' In Donne's order the similes become increasingly impersonal
and remote. *9. in*. So in several Mss. Edn. 1633 has 'on'; but the devil's
usurpation is not *on* man, but on the divine 'titles' *in* man. *10. that's*. That which
is. *13. yet will not choose me*. By refusing to 'choose' (i.e. elect to eternal life) God
lets his 'titles' go by default. Gardner keeps the 1633 monosyllabic contraction
'wilt' not' (equivalent to 'won't'). Not found in any Ms., this makes the stress
fall on *me*; but Donne speaks as a representative man, not an individual sinner.

    2. On the approach of Death.
    3–4. The figure of man as a pilgrim on earth was traditional (cf. *AS* 4.12–13).
Donne's variation, where an act of treason prevents the 'pilgrim' from returning
to his own country, adds a contemporary note. *4. whence*. The place from which.
5–8. The conceit may have been suggested by the figure of life as a prison
from which all are taken to execution, in More's *Four Last Things*. *6. delivered*.
Released. *8. be imprisoned*. 'be' elides with the first syllable of 'imprisoned'.
9–10. Repentance will win grace; but grace is first needed for the soul to
repent. *14*. Cf. Isaiah i.18: 'though your sins be as scarlet, they shall be as
white as snow.'

    3. On Death's coming.
    1–4. The images suggest a gradual constriction of space and time to the
instant of death. Contrast the gradual expansion in *ShS* 4.1–4. *1. This...scene*.
More's figure of life as a stage-play is close to one of life as a prison; but *last
scene* may recall the end of Marlowe's *Doctor Faustus*; cf. ll. 11–12 and note. *3.
pace*. Step. *4. span*. The length of the extended hand from thumb to little

finger, reckoned at nine inches. The image is biblical (Psalm xxxix.5). *minutes'*
latest point. The last minute mark on a clock face. Gardner adopts 'last' from
Mss., but this upsets the metre, and could be a slip in the first transcription of
the poem. *5. unjoint.* Disjoin, with a suggestion of breaking joints. *7. I know not.*
The earlier version. Later, for doctrinal reasons, l. 7 became 'But my ever-
waking part shall see that face', eliminating the doubt expressed. *presently.* At
once. *11. so fall.* 'So let (them) fall'. *11-12. that all...to hell.* The sins are sardoni-
cally granted repatriation in hell; but they are trying to jostle the poet with
them. The conceit resembles the finale of *Doctor Faustus. 13.* 'Imputed righteous-
ness' signified righteousness attributed (transferred) to the soul through
Christ's sacrifice and virtue. *14. the world...devil.* Renounced at baptism (Book
of Common Prayer).

4. On the Last Judgment.
1-2. At the...angels. Suggested by Rev. vii.1: 'I saw four angels standing on
the four corners of the earth'. Donne's scientific curiosity compounds 'imagined'
corners with actual 'round earth'. *5.* God covenanted that the earth would
never again be destroyed by flood (Gen. ix.11); Christian tradition held that
next time it would be destroyed by fire. *6-7. war...chance.* The catalogue shows
critical awareness of such avoidable social ills as *war, dearth, tyrannies, law.*
Many texts have 'death' (used for plagues) for *dearth,* but 'dearth' is more
likely than 'death' as a *cause* of death. *7-8. and you...woe.* (Those not already
dead on Judgment Day.) *9. a space.* For a while. *12. there.* In heaven, before the
throne of judgment. *13. Teach...repent.* Cf. **2.**9-10.

5. On Hell.
1. that tree. The tree of knowledge of good and evil growing in Eden (Gen. ii),
whose fruit tempted man to his fall. *3. goats.* Traditionally the most lecherous
of creatures. *serpents envious.* 'God said unto the serpent...I will put enmity
between thee and the woman, and between thy seed and her seed' (Gen.
iii.14-15). *envious:* malicious. Donne means natural serpents after the Fall, not
the archetypal 'serpent' Satan, who was indeed damned. *5-6.* 'An audacious,
blasphemous evasion of responsibility' (Martz 1). But Donne's protest is based
on the Augustinian doctrine that man alone is damned since the Fall by his
reason, yet cannot save himself by reason. *7. glorious.* Conferring glory. *9-14.*
'Reason emerges triumphantly...with an exact command of the theology of
redemption' (Martz 2). In view of the ending (see note to l. 13) the sestet
amounts rather to a desperate plea for oblivion. *9.* Cf. Job xl.2: 'Shall he that
contendeth with the Almighty instruct him?' *11. Lethean flood.* In Greek
mythology the souls of the dead forgot their former life when washed by the
waters of the underworld river Lethe. *13. them.* Ambiguous. The pronoun
seems to refer back to *sins,* l. 12; but what *some claim as debt* (i.e. their due) must
be God's memory of themselves as *persons;* hence *them* alludes to the *some* that
follows it. While 'some' want God to remember them, Donne wishes to be
forgotten.

6. On Heaven, or victory over Death. Donne later regretted the over-
confidence of this sonnet; the Elegy on Mistress Boulstred, written in the same
year, began: 'Death, I recant and say, unsaid by me / Whate'er hath slipp'd
that might diminish thee...'
4. yet. Moreover. *me.* My soul. *5. pictures.* Symbols, figures. *7.* 'Our best men

are the soonest to go.' *8. delivery.* Release. *11. charms.* Perhaps 'soothing songs' rather than incantations. *12. swell'st.* Taking up 'proud', l. 1, in the sense of 'swollen'. *14. death, thou shalt die.* 'Death, where is thy sting?' (I Cor. xv.)55.

7. Offering himself in place of the humiliated Jesus, Donne heavily stresses *my, me, I,* in ll. 1–3. The argument in ll. 5–8 introduces a historical relativism with awkward implications (see Introd., p. 28).

1–2. Follows the anti-Jewish tradition of the established church; in the gospel accounts all these acts were performed by Roman soldiers (Matt. xxvii.27–35, Mark xv.16–20, John xix.34); in Luke xxiii women 'bewailed him' and the people 'smote their breasts' (27, 48). *5. satisfied.* Requited. *6. pass.* Surpass. *8. being now glorified.* Refers to Christ, whose divinity was made manifest by his church. *11–14.* Traditional exegesis of the Old Testament in terms of the New. Jacob wore kid-skins on hands and neck to impersonate Esau to his blind father Isaac (Gen. xxvii.15–16); this was taken to prefigure Christ's assumption of human form. *11. vile harsh attire.* 'Goodly raiment', according to the biblical account, but altered here to suit the identification of Jacob with Christ.

8. This resembles a meditation prescribed by Loyola: 'running through all creatures in my mind, how they have suffered me to live...the elements, the fruits of the earth, the birds, the fishes, and the animals...The whole to conclude with a colloquy of mercy' (Martz 1).
2. the prodigal elements. Earth, air, fire (as sunlight), and water, all lavish in gifts. *4.* The elements were each of one kind, hence less corruptible than man who, compounded of all four, suffered from their frequent imbalance. *5. brook'st.* Bearest. *6. seelily.* Foolishly. *8. kind.* Race. *9. woe is me.* Pronounced with a slur; almost 'woe's me'. *11.* A line of five stresses without regular feet: 'But wónder at a greáter wónder; fór to ús'.

9.
2–3. Mark...crucified. Adapted from the common romance conceit that the poet has the picture of his mistress engraved upon his heart. Cf. Alabaster 3.10. *5. amazing.* Terrifying. *8. Which...spite.* Cf. Luke xxiii.34. *fierce.* Said of the 'chief priests' and a 'multitude' at the trial of Jesus (Luke xxiii.5). *9. my idolatry.* The time when Donne was dedicated to human instead of divine love. *10. profane.* Secular, unhallowed. *11. Beauty of pity.* Beauty is a sign of pity: an extension of the Renaissance Platonist view that physical beauty was a manifestation of ideal virtue. *foulness.* Ugliness. *12. thee.* His soul (following up l. 2). *13.* The folk tradition (perhaps meant by *assigned*); but contrast II Cor. xi.14: 'Satan himself is transformed into an angel of light', interpreted to mean that 'wicked spirits' could assume beautiful shapes.

10. A plea to be enabled to love God adequately, expressed in symbols whose erotic character becomes explicit in the sestet.
1–4. Characteristic in the overriding of regular metre by impetuous stress effects. The image of the heart as a besieged fortress derives from romance (cf. Surrey 1); here the assault suggests contemporary cannons and mines. *5–6.* The heart secretly sympathizes with the attacker, God, who is reclaiming his own domain usurped by Satan. *7. viceroy.* Governor of the 'fortress' of the heart. *9–14.* Erotic associations take over from fortress imagery. A craving for God's

love is identified with the romance heroine's desire to be rescued from a forced union with his enemy.

11 and **12** are from a group of four penitential sonnets added in the 1635 edition and inserted among those already printed, with the numbering 1 and 5.

11.

1. decay. Fall into destruction. *4. like yesterday.* Passed into memory. *8. it... weigh.* The weight of sin pulls the *feeble flesh* (l. 7) down to hell (conceived as the centre of the earth). *9. Only thou.* 'Thou alone'. *11. subtle foe.* Satan, theologically identified with the 'subtil' Serpent in Eden (Gen. iii.1). *13. wing.* Add wings, as in falconry feathers were 'imped' to a hawk's wing. *to...art.* To forestall Satan's wiles. *14.* The paradox lies in the *iron* hardness of the heart, which enables God to draw it up as if with a magnet (*adamant*).

12. Based on the ancient correspondence between the individual (as microcosm) and the universe (as macrocosm). Donne introduces recent geographical findings and astronomical theories, turning in the sestet to dwell on sin and punishment.

1. cunningly. Skilfully. *2. angelic sprite.* The indwelling spirit, which in man's *little world* corresponds to the angels in the empyrean or highest sphere of the macrocosm. *5–6. You...spheres.* Those who, rejecting the Copernican system, posit spheres beyond the traditional nine. The Jesuit mathematician Clavius had argued for an eleventh sphere in 1607 (Gardner). *new lands.* Notably in the Americas and Indies. *7–8.* In the microcosm tears become *new seas*, and weeping earnestly suggests a new Flood to *Drown my world. 9.* See note to **4.**5. *10. But...burnt.* Individual punishment in hell flames was a 'correspondence' to the future destruction of the world by fire. *14. thy house.* God's temple, located in man's body. (See note to **1.**8.) *eating.* Consuming with fire.

13–15. These sonnets, previously unknown, were found in a Ms. from the Earl of Westmoreland's library and first printed in 1899. They are 'occasional' rather than part of a series.

13.

1. she...loved. Assumed to be Donne's wife, Ann More, who died in 1617 at the age of 32. *1–2. her...nature.* The return of her body to earth; a traditional figure. *2. to hers and my good.* Since both are freed from earthly desire. *5. the admiring her.* Wonder at her virtues. *6. streams...the head.* Earthly love leads back to the divine fountain-head from which it springs. *the* (Gardner). Misread as 'their' by Grierson and previous editors. *7–8.* (Instead of ending the octave with the calm devotion of ll. 1–6, a note of restlessness enters in.) *8. holy thirsty dropsy.* An unquenchable, as it were morbid, thirst of the spirit. *10.* Gardner's punctuation, for the Ms. reading: 'Dost wooe my soule for hers; offering all thine'. *11–14.* The lines are in effect a quatrain, hinging on a repressed conflict. God is gently reproached for his fear that Donne might deviate into the Catholic 'error' of loving *saints and angels* (i.e. his wife), and, more significantly, for God's *tender jealousy* regarding a grosser desertion to *the world, flesh, yea, devil.* (If such 'jealousy' is absurd, why is it mentioned?)

14. Shows sceptical detachment over the claims of rival churches. The imagery develops from the figure of the church as bride of Christ to romantic and finally sexual themes.

1. thy spouse. The 'true church' (from Rev. xxi.9, 'I will show thee the bride, the Lamb's wife'). *bright and clear.* In the Vulgate rendering of Rev. xix.8, the 'wife' is arrayed in fine linen, *'splendenti et candido'. 2. on...shore.* In Catholic France. *4. Germany and here.* Countries where the Reformation had stripped the church of its ceremonial. In England Donne probably had in mind the Puritan sects. *5.* Cf. 'the seven sleepers' den' in *The Good-Morrow. 6. self.* Pristine, original. *Now...outwore?* 'Can the true church be either 'new' or 'obsolete'? *8. one hill.* Mount Moriah, site of the Jerusalem Temple (where the 'bride' is shown, Rev. xxi.9–10). *seven hills.* Rome. *no hill.* The unlocalised seat of the Reformed churches. *9. adventuring knights.* Knights errant. (Instead of marriage to the 'spouse' at a set place, the conceit suggests an undirected chivalric quest for 'romance'.) *11. Betray, kind husband.* Donne's unregenerate wit makes Christ a complaisant husband addressed by the 'adventuring knights'. *12. thy... dove.* 'Open to me...my dove, my undefiled' (Song of Solomon v.2). *13–14.* i.e. the true church is the least exclusive; but the courtly wit creates an erotic paradox.

15.
1. contraries...one. A major theme of Renaissance thought, and the philosophic aspect of the age's (and Donne's) love of paradox. *3–4.* The *constant habit* is the discrepancy between a desire for consistency and constant changes of belief. *5. humorous.* Subject to humours, traditionally choleric, sanguine, melancholy, and phlegmatic, but used loosely at this time for arbitrary urges. *6. my profane love.* Cf. 'my idolatry', **9**.9. *7. distempered.* Unbalanced. *cold and hot.* From the 'elements' which made up the body's humours. *8. As...as.* Now...now. *10. flattering.* Intended to please. *13. fantastic ague.* Fever in the 'fancy', one of the faculties of the mind, with 'understanding' and 'memory'. *here.* In this respect. *14.* His 'shaking' (cf. the name 'Quakers' given to Fox's sect) is seen as a kind of quotidian fever.

GLOSSARY

abuse (v.): deceive
affamished: starved
again: back, in return
against ('gainst): in anticipation of
allow: make allowance for
amerced: fined
amiss (n.): misdeed
antique: ancient
approve: prove
askance: sideways
assay: test, trial
assoil: discharge
assummon: summon up
astonished: dismayed

bare in hand: falsely led to believe
bark: vessel
bate (n.): discord, contention
beguiled: foiled
beshrew: cursed be
betide: befall
bit: bite
blenches: turnings away
boss: metal knob (on side of bit or bridle)
brabbling: brawling
brake: thicket
bravely: in fine clothing
brood: lineage
building: structure

carcanet: ornamental collar
care: anxiety
censures (v.): judges
chafe (n.): anger

checks: (1) rebuffs; (2) auditor's marks against items
cheer (n.): (1) expression on face; (2) disposition
chide (with): scold
clips: embraces
closet: (1) private room; (2) cabinet
comfort: support
confess: concede (in argument)
confine (n.): limit
confounds: destroys, overcomes
conquest: booty
consort (v.): accompany
conspire: combine
contrarways: in the opposite direction
convert: change
corse: corpse
counterfeit (n.): likeness
crew: company
cross (v.): frustrate
curious: enquiring:

dainty: (1) precious; (2) fastidious
dateless: unending
debate (v.): consider
deceive: cheat
deem: judge
deep: depth (of water)
demand: ask
dight: put on as clothing
disease: unrest
dressings: settings into position
dross, drossy: impurity, impure
dumpish: dejected
dun: brownish

eke: also
emprise: prowess
entertain: receive (as guest)
erst: previously
esteem (v.): estimate
estimate (n.): value
evermore: perpetual
example (v.): provide as example
extant: still alive

fain (adj.): eager
fair: beauty, beautiful
far-fet: far-fetched
figured: represented
fond(ly): foolish(ly)
forsooth: indeed
forsworn: renounced
frame (v.): give shape to

gat: begot
gaudy: joyous
ghastly: frightful
gripe: vulture (confused with eagle)

helas: alas
hideous: hateful
high: precious, rare
hind: young but full-grown female deer
hire: wages
hove: stay, remain
humblesse: humility

idle: trivial
ill-wresting: misconstruing
immured: shut or walled in
increase (n.): offspring
indifferent: impartial
indite: compose
inhearse: entomb
invention: creative power

leave: cease

liefer: more desirable
lies: resides
lieutenant: representative
lin: cease
list (v.) desire
long-settled: fixed, preoccupied
lurked: waited in ambush
lust (v.): desire (*me lusteth*: I desire)
lusty: vigorous

manners: moral character
mansion: dwelling-place
mantleth: spreads wings
masked: concealed
meed: gain, reward
merry: pleasant
methinks: it seems to me
mischance (v.): prove unfortunate
misdeem: misjudge
mortgaged: bound
mote (v.): must, might

ne: nor

offer: sacrifice
oft, often: frequent
ornament: chief adornment
owe: own

part: organ, member
parts: personal merits
pass-praise: beyond praise
pease: pacify
piece: notable example
pining: languishing
pleasance: disposition to please
port: deportment
practice: plot
prescriptions: instructions
prevent: forestall
problems: topics for intellectual dispute

prove: test
purchase: acquire, acquisition
purling: streaming
purposed: premeditated

quintessence: the invisible 'fifth essence' to be refined by alchemy; abstract significance

rack: mass of clouds
ranged: strayed
rattling: chattering
recite: declare
registers: records
remove: be absent
removed: in absence
repaired: restored
resty: lazy
review: read again
ribs: ridges
richesse: wealth
riot: dissipation
rude: rough

salve: healing ointment
scape (v.): escape
self (adj.): same
semblance: likeness
shamefast: bashful
sheeds: sheds
sheen: gleaming
silly: simple
sith, sithence: since
skill (v): know of/how
slake (v.): slacken
sluggardy: slothfulness
solemn: ceremonious
sound: unflawed
spent: worn out
spills: spoils, destroys
sprite: spirit
steem: esteem
stilts: crutches
strake: struck

stripes: lashes
subdued: subordinated
sublime (v.): refine as in a crucible
succession: descent
suffer: allow
suspect (n.): suspicion

tempers: tunes
terms: terms of years (in law)
thankless: unthanked
thereby: near there, where
thriftless: profitless
timely: early
tire: tear with beak
traffic: commerce
twain: parted

under charge: subordinate task
unfelt: unperceived
unreave: unravel

very: veritable
vouchsafe: grant

want: lack
ward: section of a prison
weed(s): attire
ween: consider
whenas: when
whoso: whoever
wights: persons
wilfully: obstinately
windlass (v.): act circuitously upon, trap
wink: close the eyes
wit: intellect, good sense
wits: intellectuals
worn: passed away
worthy: precious
wot: know
would: wish to

yield: pay as tribute